W9-CHZ-014

THE
FBI

THE
FBI

Exeter Books

NEW YORK

PAGE 1: The FBI seal.

PAGE 2, TOP: The firing line at the FBI National Academy in Quantico, Virginia.

PAGE 2, BOTTOM: The FBI crime lab handles evidence from state and local enforcement agencies.

PAGE 3, LEFT: FBI Director William Sessions (left) with CIA Director William Webster, who is also a former FBI director.

PAGE 3, RIGHT: J Edgar Hoover, FBI Director from 1924 to 1972.

RIGHT: The door to the FBI director's waiting room, 1935.

First published in USA 1989
by Exeter Books
Distributed by Bookthrift
Exeter is a trademark of Bookthrift Marketing, Inc.
Bookthrift is a registered trademark of Bookthrift Marketing, Inc. New York, New York

ALL RIGHTS RESERVED   ISBN 0-7917-0353-3   Printed in Hong Kong

CONTENTS

Introduction

America's own detective agency, the Federal Bureau of Investigation, has evolved over more than a century of jerky starts and stops, reflecting the nation's often-contradictory yearning for both liberty and justice for all. A people with a passion for fairness, domestic peace and the rule of law, Americans have demanded enforcers who will aggressively root out lawbreakers and submit them to the bounds of the society's rules. A people with an unquenchable thirst for freedom, Americans have bristled at the slightest threat of an oppressive police state that might rob them of the opportunity to shape their own destiny. In treading the fine line between the preservation of liberty and the implementation of justice, the people and their government have walked with steps variously timid and bold, reckless and cautious, weak and strong. Their footprints have worn the path that leads to today's FBI.

The trail started in 1871, when the United States Congress for the first time earmarked federal dollars for the 'detection and prosecution of crimes against the United States.' That first $50,000 allotment went to the new Justice Department, an agency created only the year before and placed under the administration of the United States attorney general. With the allocation, Attorney General Amos T Akerman organized his department for prosecutory work and appointed one detective, or 'special agent,' to conduct limited investigations for the prosecutors. All other detective work required by the department was either handled by United States attorneys and federal marshals in the field offices around the country, farmed out to investigators of other government agencies (particularly the Secret Service agents of the United States Treasury Department) or assigned to private detectives hired on a case-by-case basis.

Throughout the 1880s, United States attorneys general continued the practice of borrowing or hiring detectives from outside the Justice Department to meet the growing caseload. Attorney General Benjamin Brewster introduced the practice of routinely using men from the private Pinkerton detective agency. This practice alarmed some lawmakers, and in 1892 Congress passed a law prohibiting the use of private investigators for government work. The Justice

BELOW: Attorney General AT Akerman, the organizer of the forerunner of the FBI, circa 1870.

Department was forced to take its investigative assignments to an assortment of bank examiners, customs inspectors, and, in most cases, the Secret Service men in the Treasury Department.

As the investigative workload of the Justice Department grew, it became painfully apparent that relying on a makeshift setup of borrowed detectives was not getting the job done. By 1906, Congress approved the use of up to 32 Treasury Department Secret Service agents for temporary Justice Department assignment, subject to the year-to-year funding of the House Appropriations Committee. The Secret Service, which had been established to investigate counterfeiting 'and similar related outrages' (and, after 1907, was tasked

with providing physical security for the President of the United States), was haphazardly becoming an interagency detective pool.

Not only were Washington-based government prosecutors stymied by the lack of in-house investigators, but United States attorneys and federal marshals in the field were severely hampered by the detective-hiring restrictions. Indeed, the sluggish bureaucratic process of manning investigations weighed heaviest on the Justice Department men in the outposts farthest from the nation's capital. Cumbersome procedures required that all investigators be assigned from Washington, making it next to impossible for prosecutors in the hinterlands to move quickly in gathering evi-

BELOW: A group of secret service men at the headquarters of the Army of the Potomac in October 1862. Allan Pinkerton is seated at right.

dence. But whenever a United States attorney or a federal marshal asked to be allowed to hire his own detectives, they were denied on the grounds that there was no precedent for authorizing them to pick their own investigators.

The twentieth century brought the country a vigorous, reform-minded president intolerant of corruption and impatient with bureaucratic sludge. But when President Theodore Roosevelt began advancing his trust-busting agenda in Washington, he immediately butted heads with a suspicious Congress, many of whose members took a dim view of 'that damned cowboy' and his energetic efforts at reform. They were particularly alarmed when Roosevelt's beacon of reform was shined on government officials.

Just months after Roosevelt took office (following the death of President McKinley in 1901) Secretary of the Interior Ethan A Hitchcock raised the suspicion that General Land Office officials were involved in fraudulent sales of federal timber lands. The lands, mostly in the western United States, were supposed to be available for homesteading and closed to commercial purposes. But speculators quickly found ways to purchase the land and resell it to lumber companies at tidy profits.

A cursory investigation of the rumors confirmed Secretary Hitchcock's fear that some of his detectives at the Interior Department were unreliable, so he followed the common practice of borrowing investigators from the Secret Service ranks at the Treasury Department to man the land fraud probe. Their work proved fruitful: in 1905, United States Senator John Mitchell and United States Representative John Williamson, both of Oregon, were indicted (and later convicted) on charges of public land fraud. United States District Attorney John H Hall was also found to be involved in the scandal and was quickly tried and convicted of fraud.

Roosevelt hinted that more investigations of congressmen and government officials were in the offing. Goaded by rumors that Roosevelt was planning to use the Secret Service as a private police force to delve into the private lives of politicians who opposed the president's legislative program, Congress moved to cut off the Justice Department's major source of police manpower. Even lawmakers who were not frightened by the hysteria of a secret police force expressed reservations about the haphazard method of using the Treasury Department as a government-wide detective agency. Many congressmen were highly suspicious of detectives in general, believing them to be an unsavory lot who too often came by

ABOVE: The Standard Oil trust was depicted as an octopus in this editorial cartoon of the early 1900s.

OPPOSITE: Just months after Theodore Roosevelt took office in 1901, questions were raised about scandal in the General Land Office.

ABOVE: Secretary of the Interior Ethan Hitchcock feared some of his detectives were unreliable for investigating fraud in the land office.

LEFT: US Senator John Mitchell of Oregon was indicted on charges of public land fraud in 1905.

their criminal expertise through hands-on experience.

Roosevelt's attorney general, Charles Joseph Bonaparte, capitalized on the sleazy reputation of the detective profession as part of his argument in favor of a professional class of government investigators to be hired and trained by the Justice Department. For whatever combination of reasons, the fear of a secret police ran deep in the Congress, and the votes were there to block, at least temporarily, Bonaparte's efforts to establish in the Justice Department an agency of professional government investigators.

In 1908, Congress took the additional step of blocking the appropriation of funds to the Justice Department 'for any person detailed or transferred from the Secret Service,' thus plugging the department's last source of investigative manpower. The bill was to take effect at the beginning of the 1909 fiscal year. In a 6 May 1908 editorial, The New York Times castigated Congress for 'having become the tools of thieves.' President Roosevelt, too, was outraged. 'Only criminals need fear our detectives,' he wrote to a congressman.

But Bonaparte did not retreat. Using funds already in his department budget, the attorney general quickly hired nine Secret Service officers who had worked primarily on Justice Department cases. The men were transferred to the Justice Department payroll just days before the appropriations bill took effect. Bonaparte had met the letter of the law, but had also gotten the trained detectives he needed.

The new men joined the Justice Department's 14 special agents and examiners to form a permanent subdivision under the direction of Chief Examiner Stanley W Finch. A year later, Bonaparte's successor, Attorney General William W Wickersham, christened the new unit the Bureau of Investigation. In 1935, under the leadership of J Edgar Hoover, it would formally become the Federal Bureau of Investigation.

OPPOSITE BOTTOM: The Treasury Department in Washington, DC. Secret service men at Treasury were often used by other government departments.

RIGHT: Roosevelt's attorney general Charles Bonaparte argued for a special class of government investigators within the Justice Department.

CHAPTER ONE

THE EARLY YEARS

In the first few years, agents spent much of their time investigating peonage crimes, cases in which men or women were held in slavery to pay off their debts. With the bureau's enforcement effort, it wasn't long before the number of peonage cases fell dramatically. Other early bureau assignments involved preparing trust-busting cases, looking at banking law violations and illegal interstate shipment of liquor, locating fugitives, and investigating crimes committed on federal property. At this time agents did not have full powers of arrest and were not permitted to carry weapons except on special occasions. These restrictions, crippling to effective law enforcement, would not be lifted for more than 20 years.

The Mann Act, also known as the White Slavery Act, passed by Congress in 1910, was the first new major criminal statute that fell under the bureau's jurisdiction. Enforcement of the law fell to the Bureau of Investigation mostly by default because Congress did not specify any other agency to undertake the assignment.

The act had its roots in the early 1900s with the rising concern over the international trade in white women. European nations agreed to try to stop the traffic, and the United States joined the pact in 1908. The Mann Act forbade the transportation of women across state lines for immoral purposes. The act targeted prostitution rings that moved women from city to city, but it also disallowed crossing state lines with a woman even if she went willingly. The law contained the phrase 'any other immoral practice,' opening the door for a wide variety of legal interpretations. The law increased the federal government's jurisdiction over a variety of interstate crimes and is cited by numerous sources as the first act to open the scope of bureau activities.

RIGHT: Attorney General George Wickersham directed the new Bureau of Investigation to look into commercial vice and abuse of minors.

In later years, critics of the FBI would point to the Mann Act as an early example of law enforcement abuse, the feared infringement on liberty in the name of justice. But, at the time, Attorney General George W Wickersham instructed bureau director Stanley W Finch to concentrate on cases

ABOVE: The employees of the Department of Justice's Bureau of Investigation gather for a photo in 1913. Seated at the far right is A Bruce Bielaski, chief of the bureau.

LEFT: Chicago authorities investigate a white slavery plot in July 1926.

that clearly involved commercial vice or gross abuse of minors. Wickersham did not want to waste federal money and investigative resources tracking down love-struck teenagers running across state lines to escape their parents.

Wickersham's guidelines, however, did not prevent abuse of the Mann Act. Moralists had targeted New York as the hotbed for the nationwide white slavery problem, apparently ignoring the fact that a special grand jury headed by John D Rockefeller Jr had uncovered no evidence of organized trade in women in that city. Federal prisons filled quickly with people convicted under the Mann Act. Perhaps the best-known victim of the hysteria was Jack Johnson, the first black heavyweight boxing champion.

The style of this black champion offended the sensibilities of the times, which were marked by strict racial segregation. Johnson's major crime, apparently, was his failure to accept the role white society wanted to assign to a black boxing champion. Johnson refused to allow his blackness, or the prevailing racial mores, to restrict his lifestyle. He made a lot of money and he liked to show it off. He enjoyed a variety of public relationships with prostitutes, most of whom were white. Adding to his high profile, Johnson opened a lively bar known as Cafe de Champion in Chicago.

Johnson's legal problems began after his second wife, who was white, shot and killed herself. Shortly after the suicide, a white woman from Minneapolis named Lucille Cameron came to Johnson's bar looking for work. He hired her, gave her a place to live, and offered her friendship. But a few weeks later, Cameron's mother showed up in Chicago with her lawyer, Charley Eberstein, claiming Johnson had abducted her 20-year-old daughter.

Cameron was whisked away from Johnson's 'clutches' at his bar, and Eberstein and others held her under house arrest, although she had not been charged with anything. They tried to convince her that Johnson had committed a substantial crime and that she should assist in prosecuting him, but she refused to cooperate because, she said, Johnson had done nothing wrong. She said that she had come to Chicago on her own and had sought his help. Cameron and Johnson were later married.

Nonetheless, Chicago City Council passed a resolution denouncing Johnson, and the state of Illinois revoked his liquor license. Eberstein continued the verbal assault of Johnson through the newspapers. 'I feel that Jack Johnson has insulted every white woman in the United States,' he told reporters. 'I want to see justice done.'

The Justice Department entered the case, and investigators encouraged a jealous prostitute, Belle Schreiber, to testify that the boxer had taken her across state lines and paid her money for immoral purposes. The woman had traveled with Johnson and the boxer had helped her financially. The circumstances left him vulnerable to a law that acknowledged few fine lines.

When Johnson was tried in May 1913 on white slavery charges, he acknowledged that he had given money to Schreiber. But he insisted the money had not been given in exchange for sex. Although Johnson and Schreiber did have a sexual relationship, the champion was known to be generous with money to friends and lovers who were down on their luck.

Despite his pleas of innocence, Johnson was convicted and sentenced to one year and one day in prison and fined $1000. Many white men had been sentenced to prison under similar circumstances, but Johnson remained convinced that his prosecution

LEFT: Jack Johnson with his wife, Irene, in Paris in 1933.

BELOW: Johnson's nightclub, 'The Showboat,' opened in Los Angeles in 1931.

15

WAR WHAT FOR?
FOR PROFITS
OF COURSE!

ДА ЗДРАВСТВУЕТ
8-ЧАСОВОЙ
РАБОЧИЙ ДЕНЬ

ON MAY 1

ABOVE: War protesters demonstrate on May Day 1916.

OPPOSITE TOP: The Black Tom explosion in New York Harbor in July 1916.

OPPOSITE BOTTOM: The bridge linking the US and Canada at Vanceboro, Maine, which was dynamited by a German saboteur in 1919.

was racially motivated. Rather than submit to what he saw as unfair imprisonment, he fled the country and remained an expatriate for seven years. The case came to be regarded as a low mark in American justice, and the Bureau of Investigation took its share of notoriety from its involvement in the investigation.

The controversial white slavery issue soon subsided with the onset of world war. World War I introduced a new age, with a new set of problems. It quickly became apparent that the bureau in particular, and American society in general, were ill-prepared for change. Foremost, a nationwide effort was needed to control foreign sabotage and domestic mob hysteria. Inexperienced in these circumstances, the bureau supported measures that caused or exacerbated the individual rights abuses of the times. Even hard-core FBI supporters acknowledge it was a dismal era for federal law enforcement.

Before the United States entered the war in 1917, sabotage and spying went nearly unchecked. Few industries knew how to cope with the wartime problems, and coordination between Allied and national intelligence agencies was virtually nonexistent. And most agencies, including service intelligence divisions, were understaffed.

Explosions, many of them never explained, rocked numerous powder plants, ammunition dumps and chemical plants. One of the most spectacular happened on 30 July 1916 at Black Tom Island in New York Harbor. A dynamite explosion so huge that the noise was heard as far away as Philadelphia destroyed this key transfer point for material going to Europe. Three men and a child were killed.

In another well-publicized sabotage case, former German soldier Werner Horn dynamited the bridge linking the United States and Canada at Vanceboro, Maine, in 1919. He was convicted of transporting dynamite

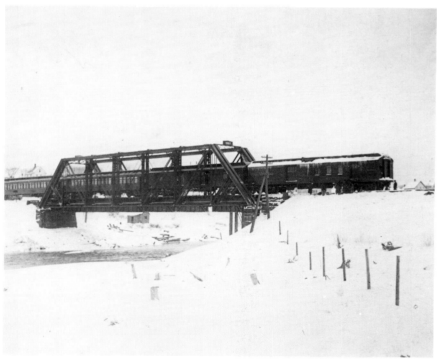

on an international passenger train. (There was no federal sabotage statute at the time.)

Bureau agents uncovered some of the details of German spying and sabotage after the United States entered the war, but much of the damage had been done by that time. Bureau agents learned of the situation when they tunneled into the Swiss consulate in New York and found boxes bound with tape and bearing the imprint of the German seal.

A Bruce Bielaski had been appointed the second head of the bureau in 1912. By the time America entered the war, his agency had grown to about 200 agents. But even with an additional increase in personnel, the bureau was far from ready to handle new duties that included checking on potentially dangerous aliens and helping round up 'slackers,' or draft dodgers. Inevitably, an increase in public hysteria over spy scares brought out a plethora of vigilantes and self-styled investigators. In some communities, people reported each other for seemingly

un-American utterances. Unofficial committees harassed or threatened those whose patriotism they considered suspect.

Bureau Director Bielaski further charged the crackling atmosphere when he sought and received from Attorney General Thomas W Gregory approval for the American Protective League. Formed by Chicago advertising executive A M Briggs, the APL was to be a volunteer organization of American citizens who were eager to help with national defense. But the group's members proved themselves to be subject to virtually no control – public or private – as they pursued their loosely-defined goals.

Hundreds of thousands of self-styled American patriots eventually joined the organization. At first, they wore badges bearing the words 'Secret Service,' although they had no official ties with that investigative wing of the Treasury Department. While many who joined the league were never active, and others proved to be sincere citizens who did meaningful and helpful work, in general the American Protective League's activities ignited outrage and stirred hundreds of reports of illegal arrests, beatings and searches.

The would-be patriots of the APL brought their outraged critics to the doorstep of the Bureau of Investigation when the citizens' organization teamed with Bielaski's agency in what became known as the 'Slacker Raids.' Bielaski was concerned about how to deal with the problem of identifying and arresting the hundreds of thousands of 'slackers' – American men who either had not registered for the draft or had dodged military induction after receiving notice. The director had experimented with using APL members to help with slacker round-ups in Chicago, Pittsburgh and Boston. He was pleased with the success of the operations, and decided to use the tactic during an ambitious three-day raid in New York, Brooklyn, Newark and Jersey City.

Although there were notices in the press reminding draft-eligible men to carry their draft classification cards at all times, there was no real warning that any sort of massive government check was coming. So it came as a shock when, just two months before the war ended, 35 special agents of the Bureau of Investigation, 2000 APL operatives, 1350 soldiers and national guardsmen, 1000 sailors and several hundred policemen swept into the four cities. The slacker hunters detained any male who was not carrying his classification card or could not show proof of his birth date. The nation that had joined the fight to make the world safe for democracy watched as its soldiers stopped citizens at bayonet point on American streets, demanding to see proper identification.

Most of the 50,000 men who were taken into custody and transported to regimental armories were held for hours without an opportunity to prove their innocence. A few thousand men were referred to draft boards for delinquency and another 1500 were drafted. The rest of the so-called slackers suffered through an unwarranted and humiliating detention. Public outcry demanded an accounting by President Woodrow Wilson, who turned the demand over to his attorney general. Gregory accepted full responsibility for the raids because, while only 35 of the 4500 persons engaged in the raids were under the direction of the attorney general, the Justice Department was accountable for the entire operation.

In later years, particularly during World War II, FBI Director J Edgar Hoover would

OPPOSITE TOP: Authorities conduct a slacker raid in the fall of 1917 in Los Angeles.

OPPOSITE BOTTOM: The New York headquarters of the American Protective League in 1919.

BELOW: Slacker raids were conducted in New York City in September 1918.

ABOVE: A ship packed with European immigrants arrives in New York Harbor.

RIGHT: Bureau of Investigation Chief William J Flynn, appointed in 1919.

point to World War I abuses such as the slacker raids as examples of why federal law enforcement should remain in the hands of trained investigators. The American Protective League was disbanded shortly after the war, and efforts to start similar organizations during the next war were resisted.

The Bureau of Investigation, however, had little time to recover from such controversies before the backwash of war brought a new round of problems. With the coming of armistice, America had defeated its enemies abroad but faced new ones at home. Fascists, communists and anarchists, real and imagined, seemed determined to disrupt government operations and American society by a variety of means. The problem was a tangible one. Communists had come to power with the revolution in Russia, and that success led to a surge in party membership in the United States. Anarchists grew bolder.

In response, xenophobia (the fear of foreigners) and anti-radicalism swept through the country. Attorney General A Mitchell Palmer and Bureau of Investigation Chief William J Flynn, both appointed to

ABOVE: Anarchists marching in a New York labor demonstration in March 1914.

LEFT: The wig, mustache and passport found in the rooms of alleged German spies in 1919.

ABOVE: Mrs Carl Muck, wife of the former leader of the Boston Symphony Orchestra, registered as an enemy alien in 1918. Her property was seized and her husband interned.

RIGHT: Attorney General A Mitchell Palmer.

OPPOSITE: Palmer's home was bombed by revolutionaries in June 1919.

Then, on 2 June 1919, nine bombs exploded in eight cities. Among the intended victims of the bombs were members of the president's cabinet, senators, members of the House of Representatives, a Supreme Court justice, state governors and influential businessmen. At almost every bombing site police found handbills declaring revolution. 'A time has come when the social question's solution can be delayed no longer; class war is on, and cannot cease but with a complete victory for the international proletariat,' the handbills declared.

Attorney General Palmer felt enormous public pressure to respond to the bombings. The attorney general needed no prodding from anyone; Palmer himself had been the target of one of the bombs. The explosion meant for him had blasted off the front of his Washington, DC home. The two bombers who had laid the dynamite were caught in their own explosion. Bloody bits of bone and body parts from the two bombers were scattered on Palmer's doorstep and strewn on his neighbors' lawns. Palmer was not hurt.

One of Palmer's first moves in the aftermath was the appointment of Justice Department attorney John Edgar Hoover to the command of the newly-created General Intelligence Division. Palmer directed Hoover to conduct an immediate study of subversives in the United States. The study quickly focused on communist groups in the United States. Hoover concluded that Moscow was the center of a conspiracy to overthrow all non-communist governments in the world, and that communist groups in

their posts in 1919, played major roles in the government's response to the postwar crisis. Another key player, John Edgar Hoover, made his grand entrance onto the stage of American public events during this period.

In 1918, Congress passed an act designed to exclude or expel aliens who were thought to be anarchists. While it was true that many of the anarchists came from the ranks of immigrants pouring into the United States, only a small percentage of these people were violent. Xenophobic paranoia, however, placed an uneasy burden on virtually all foreigners entering the United States. The first section of the law defined those to be considered anarchists and set out the basis for their exclusion from the United States. The second section allowed deportation of those already in the country who exhibited anarchistic tendencies. Like other broadly worded bills based on unreasoning fear, this was a law that seemed to invite abuse.

The situation intensified when anarchists shook the American public with a series of bombings. First, in early 1919, bombs were mailed to 29 prominent Americans. One of them exploded and hurt a servant of Senator Thomas W Hardwick of Georgia. Most, however, were found and defused.

America were an arm of that conspiracy. That reasoning was used by Hoover and other Justice Department officials to conclude that membership in certain communist groups qualified an individual for immediate deportation under the 1918 deportation act. Hoover's work quickly moved him to the forefront as a staunch foe of communism. It was a role he would play with fervor for the rest of his life.

The first roundups of aliens came in November 1919 and focused on the Federation of the Union of Russian Workers. Nearly 250 aliens were put on a transport dubbed the 'Soviet Ark' and shipped to Russia. The bureau then turned its attention to the Communist Party of America and the Communist Labor Party. Authorities declared that any member of either party was immediately deportable because both groups advocated the overthrow of the American government. Secretary of Labor William Wilson would later rescind that opinion of the Communist Labor Party. Regardless of Wilson's ruling, on 2 January 1920 mass arrest warrants were issued at Palmer's behest, and Bureau of Investigation agents fanned out in 33 cities with orders to detain anyone in the area where either of the two parties met or were presumed to meet. Agents were to gather evidence regardless of whether they had search warrants, and deportation would be based solely on membership in either party.

About 2500 people were arrested. Assistant Secretary of Labor Louis B Post sifted through the evidence and immediately began canceling warrants by the hundreds. Agents, acting under guidelines set by Palmer, had arrested mostly innocent citizens or aliens who authorities could not prove belonged to a subversive party. Authorities later determined that 446 were deported as a result of Palmer's efforts.

Questioned during investigations of the raids, Palmer steadfastly maintained that the mass roundups and deportations were justifiable in the effort to defuse the anarchist threat. The Attorney General said the situation allowed no opportunity or time to determine whether each detainee was actually a subversive. For the most part, however, Palmer's attitude reflected the depths of an ugly fear in the American public. One offspring of those days of fear and loathing was the reborn Ku Klux Klan. Dead since 1870, the Klan, a symbol of terrorism and racial hatred, was revived in the 1920s. The re-emergence of the Klan gave shape to the fears of the nation and marked another inconclusive round in the fight between liberty and justice for all.

LEFT: Immigration Commissioner Fred Wallis, left, shakes hands with Secretary of Labor William Wilson at Ellis Island.

OPPOSITE: Twenty-three communists are shown boarding ship in New York for their deportation at the height of xenophobia, in late 1919.

BELOW: The Ku Klux Klan marches in Washington, DC in 1926.

CHAPTER TWO

HOOVER AND THE BUREAU

John Edgar Hoover was born on 1 January 1895 at 413 Seward Square in Washington DC. The youngest of three children of Ann Scheitlin and Dickerson Hoover, he attended Brent Public School and Central High School. People who knew him considered Hoover a serious youth. He grew up in a religious family and once thought about becoming a minister. Religion, or at least a very moralistic interpretation of law and order, remained important to him throughout his life.

BELOW: J Edgar Hoover as an infant.

In high school, Hoover loved sports and played on the baseball team. But a sharply driven ball or a fly ball, depending on which source you believe, flattened his nose and cut short his playing days. That baseball accident created the bulldog look that later accented his image as America's top crime-fighter.

Academics proved to be his strong suit. His skill as a debater made him a leader on the school team. At graduation, he was named valedictorian of the Class of 1913. Hoover went on to George Washington University and earned his Bachelor of Law degree by 1916. His master's degree followed in 1917. He was admitted to the District of Columbia Bar that year, and on 26 July 1917 he landed a clerkship in the Department of Justice starting at $990 a year. Hoover's first employer would also be his last.

Hoover had not been at work for long when Attorney General Thomas W Gregory appointed John Lord O'Brien special assistant in charge of war work, partially in response to complaints over the civil rights abuses committed by vigilantes during World War I. Hoover was named as one of O'Brien's aides and was made a unit chief in the enemy alien registration section. His job was to flag potential saboteurs and to look for slackers, but to do it legally. He earned a reputation for being willing to take on any assignment no matter how tedious and boring it might be.

OPPOSITE: Hoover as a child, with his mother and father in Washington, DC.

A bigger break came in 1919. When the General Intelligence Division was formed, Hoover was named to head it as a special assistant to the attorney general. He helped prosecute anarchists Emma Goldman and Alexander Berkman, and eight days after they were deported submitted his report on the Communist conspiracy.

In the legal brief Hoover was assigned to prepare in 1919, the eager young Justice Department lawyer would sound the theme that would guide the rest of his public life. In the brief, he declared that the spread of communist doctrines in the United States threatened 'the happiness of the community, the safety of every individual and the continuance of every home and fireside.' Hoover said the alien doctrines that had recently revolutionized Russia 'would destroy the peace of the country and thrust it into a condition of anarchy and lawlessness and immorality that passes imagination.'

In the 39 years that passed between the brief and the publication of Hoover's *Masters of Deceit* in 1958, the director's strong anti-communist views did not waver. In his book, Hoover wrote 'Communism is the major menace of our time.

LEFT: Emma Goldman, anarchist convicted of obstructing the draft, pictured here with Alexander Berkman.

ABOVE: Emma Goldman speaking to a crowd in Union Square in New York City in 1916.

OPPOSITE: The young J Edgar Hoover had strong anti-communist views.

RIGHT: Attorney General Harry M Daugherty, who served in the scandal-ridden Harding administration, became the target of a Senate investigation.

Today, it threatens the very existence of our Western civilization.' He went on to write:

Communism is more than an economic, political, social or philosophical doctrine. It is a way of life; a false, materialistic 'religion.' It would strip man of his belief in God, his heritage of freedom, his trust in love, justice and mercy. Under communism, all would become, as so many already have, twentieth-century slaves.

. . . The Communist Party, never forget, is a state within a state. It has its own system of 'courts,' legislative assemblies, schools and press. It enforces its own laws, has its own standards of conduct, and offers its own road to Utopia. The Party member may physically reside in the United States, but he 'lives' in a communist world.

I have deep faith in the American people and in our American way of life. But I know what communism could do to us. Not because it is stronger than we are; it is not. Not because it has something better to offer; it has not.

BELOW: US President Warren G Harding and his wife.

But we may not learn until it is too late to recognize who the communists are, what they are doing and what we ourselves, therefore, must do to defeat them.

His critics, early and late, were quick to charge that Hoover's anti-communist fervor posed a threat to the civil liberties of law-abiding American citizens. For good or bad, it was on the banner of strident anti-communism that Hoover emblazoned his name for the record of American history. And it was during those first years with the bureau that he decided his soon-to-be-famous name would begin simply with 'J.'

One story (anecdotes about Hoover are mired in myth and difficult to substantiate) had it that Hoover discovered that another man by the name John Edgar Hoover lived in Washington, and that the other John Edgar Hoover had developed a reputation as a debtor. Future-Director Hoover did not want to be confused with the other man. So he shortened his first name to the initial 'J.'

Hoover's reputation for honesty apparently served him well during the scandal-ridden administration of Warren G Harding. Hoover was named assistant director of the Bureau of Investigation on 22 August 1921 at a salary of $4000 per year. He was one of the few in a relatively high position who would survive the corruption and cronyism of the Department of Justice in the Harding years. During this period, Hoover

LEFT: William J Burns, right, is sworn in as chief of the Bureau of Investigation. Burns, founder of the Burns Detective Agency, was Daugherty's hand-picked man.

continued some of his red-hunting activities but otherwise seemed to have less power than his title of assistant director would have indicated. For the most part, Harding's administration shunted him to the side where he wouldn't get in the way.

Harding was regarded even by most of his critics as a pleasant and affable man. But when he became president in 1921, he surrounded himself with his old poker-playing buddies who had helped engineer his drive to the White House. With few exceptions, one of them being Secretary of Commerce and future president Herbert Hoover, those buddies turned out to be so corrupt or self-serving that segments of the administration nearly collapsed.

The Department of Justice and its Bureau of Investigation were not among the exceptions. Attorney General Harry H Daugherty used his position for his own means. He became so powerful that Calvin Coolidge, who followed Harding when he died in office in 1923, had difficulty removing him. Upon taking office, Daugherty had quickly fired William J Flynn as director of the Bureau of Investigation and installed an old crony, William J Burns, founder of the Burns Detective Agency, an infamous strike-breaking group. Bureau employment and advancement, which had always been dependent on political connections, became more so. Agents were so protected by their political mentors that they were able to

do pretty much as they pleased. One news reporter of the time called the bureau 'a private hole-in-the-corner goon squad for the attorney general. Its arts are the arts of snooping, bribery and blackmail.'

Gaston B Means epitomized federal law enforcement at its worst. Means came to the bureau with a shady history. He had worked as an agent for Germany in 1916, hired to harass and embarrass British commerce. There are even indications that he

BELOW: Bureau investigator Gaston B Means tells a Senate Committee about his role in the Teapot Dome scandal. He also admitted investigating the private lives of congressmen and breaking into congressional offices.

RIGHT: Albert Fall (left), former head of the Interior Department, arrives at a District of Columbia court in 1929 to face bribery charges related to oil reserve leases.

BELOW: An editorial cartoon depicting the Teapot Dome scandal of the Harding administration.

JUGGERNAUT.

was a double agent. In 1917 he was charged with the murder of Maude A King, a rich widow shot to death in North Carolina. Means was acquitted, but was later discovered to have filed a forged will that would have put him in control of Mrs King's estate.

Nonetheless, Burns hired Means as a special agent. Reaction to the hiring soon forced Burns to fire Means, but he immediately rehired him as an informant. In 1924, Means told Senate investigators that he had investigated the private affairs of senators and representatives who attacked Daugherty. He admitted to breaking into their offices and personal files, and to reading congressional mail.

Means associated with Jesse Smith, a close friend of Daugherty and a shadowy character who had no official position but who maintained an office at the Department of Justice nonetheless. (Smith committed suicide in 1923 rather than face graft and bribery charges.) Department of Justice scandals, of course, were but a portion of the Harding administration's corruption. Harding's short stay in the Oval Office became best known for the Teapot Dome scandal. Secretary of the Interior Albert B Fall allowed private contractors to pump and store naval oil reserves from the Teapot Dome oil field in Wyoming. Suddenly, neighbors and friends noticed a sharp improvement in Fall's financial situation, including costly improvements to his New Mexico ranch. The contractors involved later said they 'loaned' Fall the money. The hour struck for the entire administration shortly thereafter when Smith committed suicide, and on 2 August 1923, Harding fell ill during a trip to Alaska and died.

In 1924, Senator Burton K Wheeler of Montana sponsored a resolution that led to a Senate investigation of Daugherty's office. In response, a Montana grand jury indicted Wheeler on charges that he took money for favors from a syndicate of oil prospectors. Wheeler eventually was acquitted by a jury and the circumstances suggest that he was framed by Burns, Daugherty and the Republican National Committee.

Daugherty had taken his last shot and Burns was on his way out. Calvin Coolidge asked for and received Daugherty's resignation on 28 March 1924, just 27 days after the Senate voted to investigate the attorney general's office. J Edgar Hoover was about to start his 48-year reign over an organization that he would build into one of the world's top investigative agencies.

ABOVE: President Calvin Coolidge making his speech of acceptance in August 1924.

TOP LEFT: Senator Burton K Wheeler of Montana led the Senate investigation of Daugherty. As a result, Wheeler was indicted by a Montana grand jury on trumped-up charges but was later acquitted.

ABOVE: The new chief of the Bureau of Investigation, J Edgar Hoover, in 1924.

OPPOSITE TOP: Hoover ran the Bureau with an iron hand, and demanded that his agents be well-groomed and fit. Here, members of a District of Columbia federal grand jury view Bureau gymnasium activities in 1935.

OPPOSITE BOTTOM: The FBI baseball team meets the Baltimore Police Department team in July 1935.

Matters moved quickly. Coolidge needed intelligent, honest men for his new cabinet. Harlan Fiske Stone was the man Coolidge recruited for his Department of Justice. Stone was a high-powered New York lawyer and the former dean of the Columbia University School of Law. Although some despised him for it, he also was remembered for his criticism of Palmer's Red Raids and for defending conscientious objectors during World War I. In 1925, he would be named to the United States Supreme Court. He was the type of cabinet member Coolidge needed following the Harding years. Stone in turn needed a hard-working, conscientious man with a talent for administration to clean up his Bureau of Investigation. J Edgar Hoover's reputation had survived seven tumultuous years in the Department of Justice and he quickly became the leading candidate, although Stone apparently knew little of him at first. Stone mentioned at a cabinet meeting that he needed a director and Secretary of Commerce Herbert Hoover mentioned it to his aide, Larry Richey. Richey suggested J Edgar Hoover, and Herbert Hoover passed the name back to Stone.

On 10 May 1924, the day after Burns resigned as director of the bureau, Stone called the assistant director to his office. Stone had been cleaning house and Hoover didn't know what to expect. He was understandably nervous. 'Throughout my seven years' service in the Justice Department, I had consistently done my best. I had

nothing to hide. Nonetheless, was I to be next?' Hoover recalled in a newspaper column he wrote in 1961.

Stone, a physically intimidating man, told Hoover to sit down. After several moments of unnerving silence, Stone said, 'You're 29 years old. Some people think that's too young. I disagree. Young man, I want you to take charge of the Bureau of Investigation.' Hoover thought a moment and then agreed, but only under certain conditions. Hoover told Stone that employment and advancement at the bureau would have to be based on merit, not on political connections. And the bureau would be answerable only to the attorney general.

Hoover briskly set about remolding the bureau. He fired employees who did not meet his standards and he started his code of conduct and dress for agents. For years to come, Hoover would hire only those with a law or accounting degree to be agents. Dress was to be neat and agents were not allowed to drink. After prohibition ended, that rule was modified and Hoover himself drank moderately – but only after it was legalized again in the 1930s. Office work was standardized and bureau chiefs were given more power and responsibility. Hoover also officially purged Gaston B Means from the bureau's employment rolls. The expulsion did not, however, prevent Means from coming back to haunt the bureau a few years later.

Over the ensuing years, Hoover's list of regulations grew enormously, prompting some to ridicule the time agents wasted worrying about whether they were violating some obscure bureau rule. And Hoover did not brook any violation. Agents who incurred his wrath, no matter how minor the violation might seem, were fired or sent to some 'Siberian' post such as Butte, Montana. Others, including retired agents, have argued that Hoover's strict regimen created a sense of family and purpose among the majority of agents. In 1924 there seemed to be no question that if the bureau was to survive, it needed an iron hand of guidance.

These were not the glory and fame years that would come later. Neither Hoover nor Stone wanted a high-profile bureau that drew a lot of attention. Paranoia about a police state has always run deep in American thinking, and the recent abuses by the federal government, including the bureau, still weighed heavily. There had been serious talk of disbanding the bureau, so the main struggle in Hoover's first years was to show Congress and the public that the bureau could be run cleanly and without threatening the rights of average citizens.

By most accounts Hoover, working with Stone and the next attorney general, John G Sargent, accomplished all of the above. The irony of the situation became apparent later. Hoover, the man who succeeded in purging the system of political cronyism, would come to depend on his political connections to build his power and, eventually, to keep his job. Without question, he became one of the most powerful political men in American public affairs. But for the time being, Hoover settled in quietly to build what would become one of the best known and highly respected police agencies. Prior to his promotion, headlines about the Bureau of Investigation had centered on draft dodgers, red raids, scandals and office politics. In the face of such large issues, it was easy to forget the daily dangers the special agent in the field faced.

If any of those agents, or members of the public, needed a reminder, it came on 11 October 1925 when Agent E C Shanahan was shot to death in Chicago by a professional car thief. The 31-year-old Shanahan was the first bureau agent killed in the line of duty. He had joined the bureau in 1920. Shanahan had been on the trail of Martin James Durkin and had finally caught up with him. But as he moved in for an arrest, Durkin pulled a pistol from his car seat and shot Shanahan in the chest. Agents were not empowered to carry guns, and there was no law allowing the federal government to prosecute a man for killing a federal agent.

The bureau could, however, help track Durkin, a task made more difficult by the lack of coordination between various police agencies. Authorities followed the killer's trail through California, Arizona, New Mexico and Texas, and agents eventually found that he and his girlfriend had purchased tickets on a train to St Louis. Agents met the train at a station just outside St Louis and captured Durkin before he could reach for the guns he had in his coat. Durkin was convicted in state court and received 30 years in prison for killing Shanahan and 15 years for a series of car thefts. He was released from prison in 1954.

Shortly after Shanahan's murder, the bureau started its Fugitive Unit to coordinate efforts to catch felons who fled across state lines to avoid capture. A few years later, legislation was enacted to make the killing of a federal agent a federal crime. The bureau's duties during the era included investigating the numerous scandals left over from the Harding days. Bureau agents helped get the goods on Colonel Charles R

BELOW: John G Sargent at his desk after being sworn in as attorney general in 1925.

Forbes, the first administrator of the Veteran's Bureau. Forbes was involved in bureau kickback and payoff schemes too numerous to mention. He eventually went to prison for two years and paid a $10,000 fine for illegally disposing of $400,000 in surplus war supplies including unused material badly needed by the Public Health Service.

Agents also investigated the Atlanta federal prison, where Warden A E Sartain and a friend were convicted of accepting bribes from prisoners in exchange for soft jobs or privileges. Among those privileges was the right to gather at the warden's garage and play poker. Extensive reforms followed the investigation. Other agents uncovered graft within the Cincinnati police

department and an extortion racket among prohibition agents in nearby villages. Forty-eight police officers and 23 dry agents were indicted, and of the 70 who were tried, 62 were convicted.

In 1926, bureau agents working with local police and Border Patrol officers helped stop an invasion of Mexico that started on American soil. Former Mexican Secretary of War Enrique Estrada formed a small band of men and gathered weapons and supplies. Officers stopped the army as it prepared to leave from Southern California one night. The brass went to jail and paid fines, while most of the troops were allowed to return home.

The Bureau of Investigation of the 1920s

BELOW: Former Mexican Secretary of War Enrique Estrada, who planned an invasion of Mexico, shown here with a group of soldiers.

ABOVE: William K Hale, center, with his daughter (left) and wife. He was accused of murdering several members of the Osage Indian tribe in order to obtain head rights to their oil-rich land.

OPPOSITE TOP LEFT: Lizzie Q, an Osage Indian allegedly killed by Bill Hale.

OPPOSITE BOTTOM LEFT: Mollie Burkhart, a wealthy Osage widow, believed to have been murdered by Hale.

was publicity-shy compared to its standards of later years. But every now and then it hit the headlines with a big case, such as that of William K Hale, in which the bureau stopped a murder-for-profit spree that would have been a shocker even among today's mind-numbing horrors. The tale has been well-documented in books, newspapers and in an *American Magazine* article by Courtney Riley Cooper, who wrote more than 20 pieces about Hoover and the Bureau.

Bill Hale was a native Texan who moved to Fairfax, Oklahoma, in the middle of Osage Hills country. The area was heavily populated by Indians and infested with fugitive bandits who could evade the law by hiding in its hills and caves. The atmosphere suited Bill Hale perfectly.

Hale apparently started his career in Oklahoma by stealing cattle from the Osage Indians and selling the meat back to them. Then Hale discovered a scheme that would advance his fortunes far faster than cattle rustling. One day when he went to collect a small bill from an Osage, he found the man had died. Hale got a lien against the man's

property, claimed the man owed him thousands, and then took all the man's possessions. It was a ploy that was to be repeated time and again. Indians and any white man who might move to protect them died mysterious and violent deaths. Hale became quite wealthy.

The conditions worsened when oil was found and the Osage who owned that land became, for a while, the richest people per capita on earth. Hale prospered while they were alive by selling them cars and other luxuries and he prospered when they died, leaving him the head rights to their oil-rich land. According to various accounts, an Indian named Charlie Whitehorse was found with two bullets in his head. Another died frothing at the mouth and two others, including the great Osage cowboy Bill Stepson, died mysteriously, possibly from poisoned whiskey.

The death toll mounted until it led to bureau intervention and the downfall of Hale. Old Lizzie, who was a full-blooded Osage, owned land that would be worth an unknown fortune, and her three daughters also shared in the head rights. One of the

after Roan Horse was murdered, an explosion destroyed a house in Fairfax. Dead in the explosion was Rita Smith, another one of Lizzie's daughters; Bill Smith, her husband; and a maid. The only heir left to Lizzie's head rights was Mollie Burkhart, wife of Ernest. And she was fading slowly from an unknown ailment, alleged to have been poison.

BELOW: William Stepson was believed to have died from poisoned whiskey.

daughters, the one who would inherit the head rights if all the others died, was married to Ernest Burkhart, Hale's nephew.

Another daughter, Anna Brown, was found shot to death in a ravine near Fairfax in 1921. Then Lizzie died, apparently of natural causes, two months later. Brown's cousin, Henry Roan Horse, was found shot to death in his car outside Fairfax in 1923. Hale picked up $25,000 from an insurance policy he had on Roan Horse. Two months

After the blast that killed the Smiths, the Osage Tribal Council appealed to the federal government for help. It was determined that the bureau could assist if any of the murders happened on government land. The ensuing investigation lasted for three years. Collecting information was difficult. Hale ruled the land, and people knew what had happened to others who defied him. So four newcomers wandered into town; a cattle buyer, an insurance salesman, an oil prospector and an Indian herb doctor. All were bureau agents. It was one of the few times Hoover would send agents out undercover.

The investigation settled on the Henry Roan Horse murder because he was killed on government land. Information led the agents to a convict in the Oklahoma State Penitentiary, who sent them to another felon in the Kansas State Penitentiary. He told them to talk to Burkhart, Hale's nephew. Hale's wall of protection was about to crumble.

Burkhart broke down and told the agents the names of the men who killed Roan Horse and the Smiths, and he told them that Hale had hired them. The Smiths' killer, in fact, was already dead, set up by Hale. 'Ace' Kirby, tipped by Hale after the explosion that killed the Smiths, went to a nearby town to rob a grocer of diamonds he kept in his store. He crept into a window designated by Hale, and the grocer killed him with a shotgun blast. Hale had been to the store ahead of Kirby and told the store owner he had learned of a robbery plot. Then he told the businessman which window the robber would use.

Hale was eventually charged with Roan Horse's murder, but it took four trials to put him in prison. The first trial ended in conviction, but a Federal District Court ruled that the government had no jurisdiction over the case. The Supreme Court reversed that decision. The second trial ended in a hung jury after a defense witness committed perjury. The third trial ended in a conviction, but was reversed when an appeals court ruled it had been held in the wrong district. In the fourth trial, in 1929, Hale was convicted and sentenced to life in prison.

Americans over the years have reveled in tales of machine-gun-toting G-Men shooting it out with the bad guys, of high-speed car chases and of agents shadowing Nazi spies or communists. But despite that image, the bureau grew to depend on technology for its investigations. Tales of laboratory tests, fingerprint analysis and evidence technicians don't make headlines. But the FBI, and police agencies in general,

break more cases through careful evidence analysis and seemingly endless interviews than through bloody shootouts. Hoover himself enjoyed the G-Man image for a time, but he also spent countless hours trying to emphasize the scientific crime-busting side of his bureau. Under Hoover the bureau developed the nation's premier crime labs.

In 1924-25 the Bureau established a central fingerprint file that would become known as the FBI Division of Identification and Information. An important system that had been chaotic and piecemeal started becoming organized. The notion of establishing central fingerprint files did not originate with Hoover, but it was Hoover, with the help of Attorney General Harlan Fiske Stone, who made it a reality. Hoover and Stone's infamous predecessors, Attorney General Harry M Daugherty and Bureau Chief William J Burns, had tried to push through the same idea, but had been unable to get the necessary money from Congress.

Fingerprints had long been recognized as being so distinctive that no two are ever the same. But it was not until the early 1900s that police agencies started putting them to use to identify criminals. Before fingerprints, most used the Bertillon method, a system of minute body measurements and descriptions designed by Frenchman Alphonse Bertillon in the 1880s. The system was cumbersome and it wasn't long before officials realized that two people, even two with the same name, could look alike and have nearly identical measurements. The Bureau of Investigation got its first appropriation, a total of $56,320, from Congress for a central criminal identification department in 1924. By that time, the various branches of the armed services had fingerprint records on its men. In addition, the International Association of Chiefs of Police had its own files collected from members and the Department of Justice had records for federal and state prisons, housed at Leavenworth and worked by prisoners, who

ABOVE: The FBI's fingerprint department, one of the earliest clearing houses for evidence.

OPPOSITE: Henry Roan Horse's death led to Hale's undoing. Hale was sentenced to life in prison in 1929.

were not above changing some of the files.

Hoover had his favorite story about the value of fingerprint records and it came early in the life of the identification bureau. On 23 May 1928 four men walked into the First National Bank of Lamar, Colorado, drew guns and collected more than $200,000. A N Parrish, the bank's president, pulled a gun and shot one of the robbers. The robbers then killed Parrish, shot his son, and took two employees hostage. One was pushed out of the getaway car alive, but the other was found shot to death a short time later. The robbers also abducted a Kansas doctor and shot him to death after he treated their wounded companion. The doctor's car would lead to the solution of the case.

Although the bandits apparently tried to wipe their fingerprints off the car, a Garden City, Kansas, Police Department fingerprint expert found a partial print on the outside of a rear window. Modern fingerprint records are computerized, but in those days a hand search was required. Realizing the futility of looking through the two million records on file at the time, Hoover ordered his fingerprint men to memorize the print.

Meanwhile, four men were arrested for the robbery and Lamar citizens testified they could identify the men as the bandits. More than a year later, bureau fingerprint expert Albert B Ground was making a routine check on fingerprints from a California train robbery suspect identified as William Harrison Holden. The fingerprint check showed the man actually was Jake Fleagle, who had served time in Oklahoma for robbery. Ground went to the files several times before he discovered a match – Fleagle's right index print was the same as the one lifted from the doctor's car following the Lamar holdup. Bank robbery was not a federal crime at the time, so the discovery was sent back to the proper local authorities. But within months, police had identified all four robbers. Fleagle, who was free by that time, was killed in a shootout with police and his three accomplices were convicted and hanged. The four innocent suspects were released.

It was not the first time, nor would it be the last, that evidence analysis cleared a suspect. The fingerprint files have suffered through their share of controversy. Some police chiefs fought the centralization under the bureau in what was basically a political turf battle. And the scope of the files has come under fire over the years. When Hoover instituted programs to get people to submit their fingerprints voluntarily to the bureau, some politicians and citizens criticized the idea as part of a plan to mold the bureau into a national secret police.

OPPOSITE: Taking fingerprints at the FBI offices.

BELOW: Mug shots of bank robber and murderer Jake Fleagle, whose conviction hinged on fingerprints.

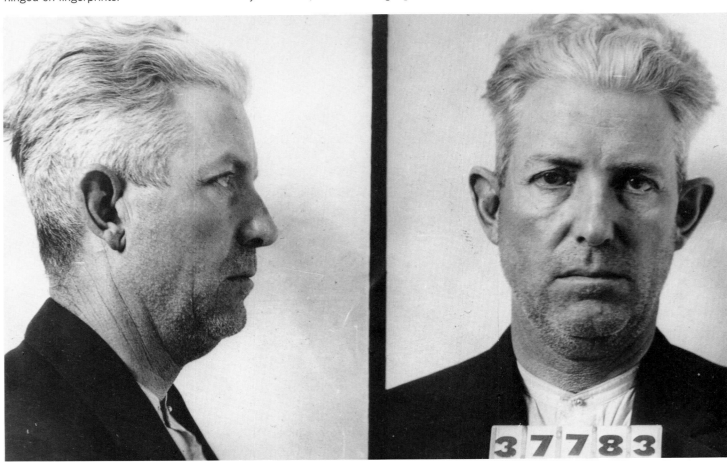

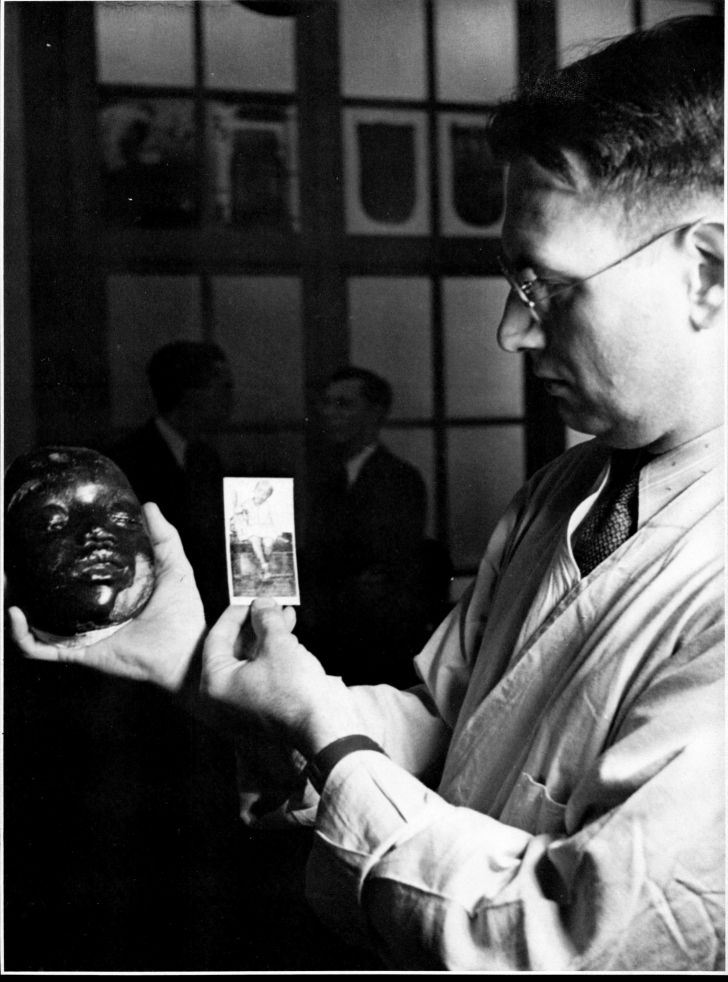

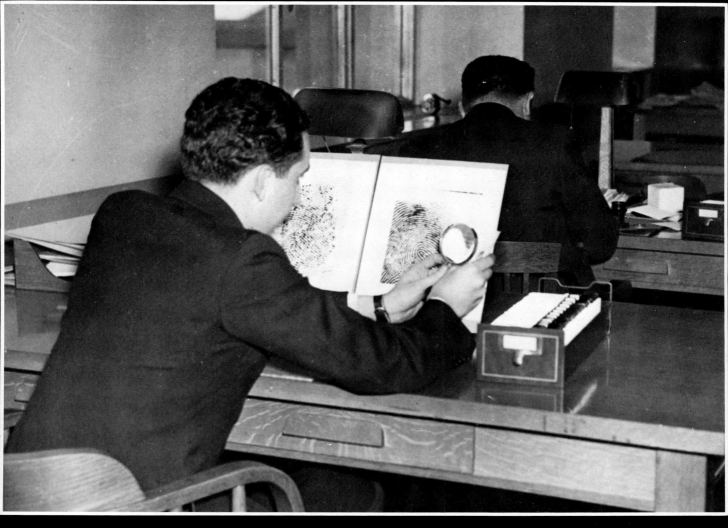

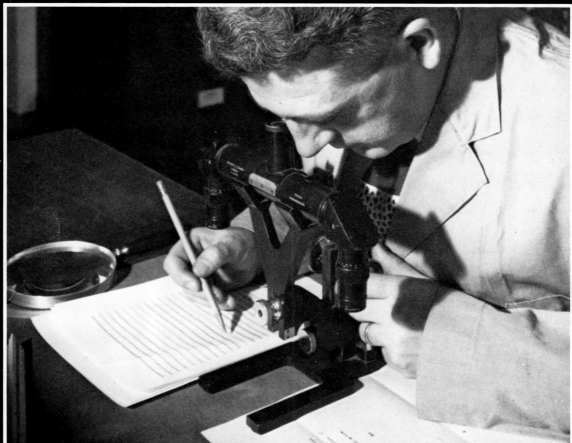

ABOVE: A fingerprint expert examines a sample from Department of Justice files.

RIGHT: A technician at the FBI laboratory analyses handwriting samples.

OPPOSITE: An official at the FBI crime lab examines a sculpture made from the photo of a murdered child.

But Hoover always fought the idea of a national police force. In 1936, he said in a letter to a newspaper that the 'secret of crime eradication lies not in a national police force but in solidarity and the combined linking of all law enforcement agencies.' Today, the FBI fingerprint files contain prints mainly from people who either submitted them voluntarily or from government employees who must be fingerprinted as part of their terms of employment.

Hoover followed the establishment of the central print files with the start of the FBI Laboratory in 1932 and the National Academy to train officers in 1935. In addition, the Fugitive Division was established in 1927 and in 1930 Congress authorized the bureau to collect and share criminal identification and other crime records with state and local authorities. That move eventually blossomed into the National Crime Information Center, a computerized service that local police can use to check for records or warrants on anyone they have detained. NCIC checks are now commonly made in many localities.

In retrospect, probably the biggest crime story of the 1920s was the rise of the gangster, fueled by thirsty throats during Prohibition. Chicago, of course, had the most notorious gangster reputation and not without cause. In the mid-1920s, more than 90 gangland murders happened there. Al Capone was free to do as he pleased and the public came to worship and glorify the gangster. Americans have always needed their heroes and the gangster filled that need. It would be another 10 years before Hollywood's 'G-Man' would displace the hoodlum.

The Bureau of Investigation was virtually powerless to fight the gangsters in the 1920s. Federal laws simply did not cover most of their activities and the Treasury Department had territorial control over liquor violations. The bureau actually nabbed Capone once for failure to appear as a witness in a federal Prohibition case, but he got only six months in jail on a contempt of court conviction. The Internal Revenue Bureau finally nailed him on income tax evasion charges, and even that conviction brought catcalls from a public amused that the federal government could do no better against someone like Capone.

Still, it would be the mid-1930s before Congress would provide laws that would allow the bureau to effectively work against kidnapers, bank robbers, car theft rings and murders.

TOP: Mug shots taken in 1931 of famed Chicago mobster, Al Capone.

OPPOSITE TOP: An FBI lab technician examines clothing for the presence of foreign matter, such as hair or fibers.

OPPOSITE BOTTOM: A technician examining automotive paint files at the FBI lab.

CHAPTER THREE

MACHINE GUN DAYS

Hero worship in the United States is sometimes hard to understand. At various points in the nation's history, statesmen, woodsmen, millionaires, homerun sluggers, space travelers, cowboys, corporate magnates, film actors, scientists, singers, preachers, puppets, cartoon characters and countless others have been objects of adulation by the American public. During the 1920s and early 1930s, that page in the country's family album marked by bathtub gin and soup lines, many Americans came to admire, even worship, the gangster.

Prohibition, in the minds of many Americans, made law-breaking acceptable, even fashionable. The federal ban on liquor proved to be a most unpopular law; government officials soon learned that reports of the death of John Barleycorn, like that of Mark Twain, had been greatly exaggerated. Not surprisingly, the professional criminals who built vast financial empires on the foundation of bootlegging cartels became folk heroes to the thirsty populace. Likewise, the less-organized (often downright inept) law enforcement officers who tried to plug the flow of contraband booze were looked upon as villains or, at best, patsies.

In the late 1920s and early 1930s, Hollywood filmmakers had discovered that gangsters and violence made good box office. In such movies as *Little Caesar* (1930) and *Public Enemy* (1931), criminals were portrayed as misunderstood heroes while lawmen were depicted as villains. The success of the 'good gangster' film genre underscored the mysterious public popularity enjoyed by American criminals at the time.

The years of corruption during the administration of Warren G Harding, some observers contend, had the effect of desensitizing the public to crime. Adventurers who outfoxed the cops in order to supply a willing clientele with a steady supply of strong drink hardly seemed as bad as government officials who stole from the public till, according to the conventional wisdom of the day. Gangsters filled the public's need for heroes who led lives filled with excitement and adventure. Yet in a few short years, the public would be easily persuaded to replace their swashbuckling gangster idols with a new hero: the G-Man.

In the early dawn of the gangsters' heyday, the Bureau of Investigation played no role in fighting booze runners. There simply were no major federal laws on the books that allowed bureau agents to join the battle of the bottle. Liquor violations were handled by the Treasury Department's Prohibition Bureau, and many of the agents of that division were corrupted by the enormous amounts of money to be made simply by turning their backs at the right time and place. (Profits from bootlegging and related activities for the Chicago gangs alone ran into the hundreds of millions of dollars.) By the time the Justice Department took control of the Prohibition Bureau in the 1930s, the last call had been sounded on Prohibition. The act was repealed in 1933.

The laws were also inadequate to equip bureau agents to respond effectively when gangsters moved beyond booze and the speakeasy and took up bank robbery and kidnaping, crimes that became almost hobbies for some mobsters. Federal, state and local authorities had neither the legal tools nor the network of interagency cooperation necessary to react quickly.

The career of George R 'Machine Gun' Kelly was typical, although he never killed a man and certainly was less savage than others of his time. Born in Tennessee in 1897, Kelly apparently tried a legitimate

ABOVE: Actor Edward G Robinson, right, in the gangster movie *Little Caesar* (1930).

LEFT: Federal agents confiscating distillery equipment during Prohibition.

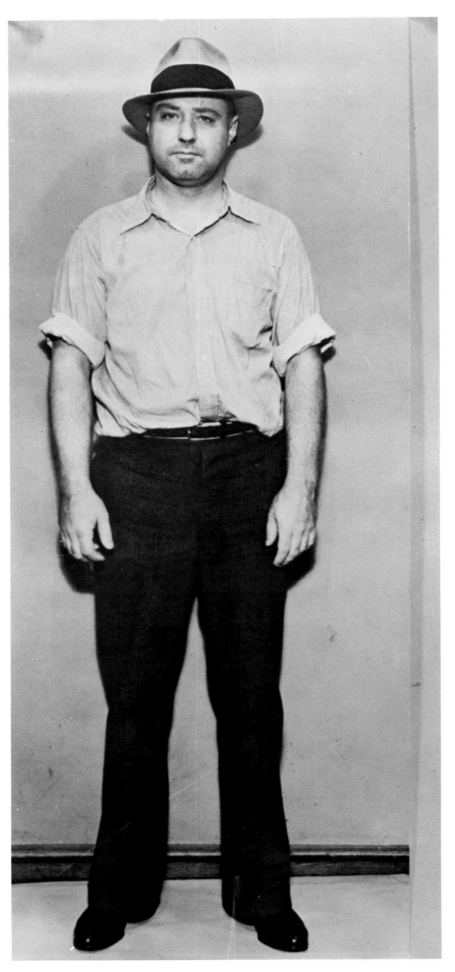

career as a salesman for a while. He turned to bootlegging in the 1920s and operated in Tennessee, New Mexico and Oklahoma. He served time in all those places, but never was in prison or jail for long.

He married Kathryn Coleman Thorne in 1927 and apparently she pushed him to move into the big time. She bought him a machine gun and his aim became deadly as he practiced by shooting walnuts off a fence. At his wife's behest, Kelly took to robbing small banks, but that yielded only tiny payoffs. So on 22 July 1933, Kelly, his wife, and a hood named Albert Bates kidnaped Oklahoma City millionaire Charles F Urschel, demanding $200,000 in ransom.

After botching the ransom pickup once, Kelly finally got his hands on the money, released Urschel, and then he and his wife went on a drunken spending spree. FBI agents and local detectives quickly found the Texas ranch where the Kellys had kept Urschel, and they arrested Kelly's in-laws, who owned the ranch. They traced Bates to Denver and soon were on the Kellys' trail to Memphis.

A bureau legend was born when agents and Memphis police broke into the Memphis flophouse where the Kellys were hiding. Hoover later told the press that Kelly cowered in a corner wimpering, 'Don't shoot, G-Man' when agents broke in, hence the start of the G-Man nickname. Kelly probably was cowering, for he never really took to the big-time criminal life, but it is almost certain that he never uttered that immortal phrase. The more plausible account of the arrest has Kelly saying, when a Memphis cop stuck a shotgun in his gut, 'I've been waiting for you.' Bates and the Kellys were all sentenced to life in prison.

Hoods such as John Dillinger and Kelly did rise to something of a cult hero status, but it was the sorts of crimes they committed that finally helped turn the public away from worship of the gangsters. As long as they were providing booze and killing each other, there was little harm done. But when they started kidnaping and killing common citizens, and when they started robbing banks of John Doe's life savings, the fun was definitely over.

Two other major crimes – the kidnaping and murder of Charles A Lindbergh Jr and a shootout known as the Kansas City Massacre – would push the public and the lawmakers over the edge and shake them from their fascination with the gangster. The Bureau of Investigation was about to acquire a public image for the first time.

The Depression was full upon the nation and 'exciting' tales of the exploits of gangsters had begun to wear thin. Then came the Lindbergh kidnaping, a crime so hideous to the average citizen that the outcry for federal intervention became irresistible. Charles A Lindbergh truly was the embodiment of the American dream. His solo trans-Atlantic flight to France had earned him fame and riches. America embraced him as royalty. The American public, and to a lesser extent the whole world, following Lindy's every move and utterance in the press. When Charles A Lindbergh Jr was born in 1930, the nation delighted in the new addition to the royal family. So when the Lone Eagle's 20-month-old baby boy was kidnaped from his crib at the Lindbergh home near Hopewell, New Jersey on 1 March 1932, the crime struck at the soul of the American public.

The federal government had no jurisdiction when the kidnaping happened. President Herbert Hoover eventually pledged the help of all government organizations, but it was obvious that most officials had not caught on that the public was looking to them for help. Attorney General William D Mitchell said the bureau would stay in close touch with authorities in case some federal statute had been violated, a waffling statement that probably brought little peace of mind. Because it was outside their jurisdiction, the Bureau of Investigation actually had little to do with the investigation or solution of the Lindbergh kidnaping. But the case is important in the bureau's history because of the legal changes it helped bring about.

The child was taken sometime in the early night. The kidnaper put a homemade ladder against the Lindbergh's house, climbed to the second floor, and spirited the boy away. This strange note was found on the windowsill:

Dear Sir

Have 50000$ ready 25000$ in 20$ bills 15000$ in 10$ bills and 10000$ in 5$ bills. After 2-4 days we will inform you were to deliver the money We warn you for making anyding public or for notify the police. The child is in gut care . . .

A month later, a retired school principal who was acting as intermediary turned $50,000 over to a man at a prearranged meeting place, and was told the boy could be found on a boat near Martha's Vineyard, Massachusetts. The child wasn't there.

As days turned to weeks and weeks to months with no break in the case, public anger and frustration with police led to massive manhunts and innumerable claims by people who said they knew where the baby

was. Mexican authorities searched trains and cars coming into the country, and some in the United States started calling for a private national police agency. As had happened during World War I when the public felt the government wasn't doing enough, vigilantes started appearing. People were certain that the underworld somehow was involved.

Swindlers also appeared, led by that shadowy figure of the early 1920s, Gaston B

ABOVE: Millionaire Charles Urschel, a kidnap victim, and his wife.

OPPOSITE: Notorious criminal Machine Gun Kelly, who kidnaped Urschel in 1933.

ABOVE: Charles A Lindbergh and his plane, the *Spirit of St Louis*, in 1927.

RIGHT: Charles A Lindbergh, Jr, kidnap/murder victim.

ABOVE: The Lindbergh home from which Charles, Jr, was kidnaped on 1 March 1932.

LEFT: The ransom note.

TWO CENTS in New York City | THREE CENTS | FOUR CENTS

LINDBERGH BABY FOUND DEAD NEAR HOME; MURDERED SOON AFTER THE KIDNAPPING 72 DAYS AGO AND LEFT LYING IN WOODS

Means. Mrs Evalyn Walsh McLean, a wealthy Washingtonian who wanted to do her part to break the case, called on Means. She apparently knew of his past and figured he had underworld connections who could assist. Means quickly convinced McLean that he did indeed know something about the case, and it wasn't long before he told her he had made contact with the kidnapers and needed $100,000 to pay the ransom. He later got another $4000, and she was preparing to hock her jewels to raise more when the bureau discovered the ruse and stepped in. Means later insisted he had made desperate attempts to find the baby. Hoover told Means he was a liar. 'Well, you've got to admit that it made a whale of a good story,' Means replied. Means and a confederate were convicted of conspiracy to commit larceny and Means was sentenced to 15 years in prison.

The agony of uncertainty for the Lindberghs and for the nation ended tragically on 12 May 1932, when a truck driver's helper stumbled on a shallow grave not far from the Lindbergh's home. Inside the grave was the body of Charles A Lindbergh Jr, his little skull crushed.

The clue that broke the case came more than two years after the kidnaping. Walter Lyle, a gas station attendant in the Bronx, noted that a man paid him for gas with a $10 gold certificate. Gold certificates were no longer in use and he remembered a flyer asking people to look out for gold certificate bills, since the kidnaper had been paid with gold certificates. He jotted down the license plate number of the car on the bill. When the bill went to the bank, a teller saw it and noted the license number. He checked the bill against the numbers of the Lindbergh ransom notes and discovered it was on the list. He called the Treasury Department.

Treasury officials and New York police traced the car to Richard Bruno Hauptmann of the Bronx, and the arrest was made. Throughout his sensational murder trial, during his appeal, and up until the moment of his execution in the electric chair on 3 April 1936, Hauptmann maintained his innocence.

The Lindbergh case was one of several that stunned federal officials into realizing they had few means to cope with interstate crime. Three months after the kidnaping Congress, despite a distinct lack of enthusiasm from Attorney General Mitchell, passed the Lindbergh Kidnap Law, which set the death penalty for transporting a kidnaped person across state lines. But that bill contained no presumptive clause, which would automatically make something a

ABOVE: Attorney General Homer Cummings, seated far right, with the members of the Lindbergh kidnaping investigation team, 1934.

LEFT: The Lindbergh Baby Trial: Accused kidnaper/murderer Richard Bruno Hauptmann, flanked by his wife on the left and a deputy sheriff. He was convicted and sentenced to death in 1936.

OPPOSITE TOP: Mrs Evalyn Walsh McLean and her attorneys testified before a grand jury in 1932 concerning hoax charges against Gaston B Means, who procured ransom money from Mrs McLean by claiming he had connections with the Lindbergh baby's kidnapers.

OPPOSITE BOTTOM: The New York Times announces the finding of the Lindbergh baby's body in May 1932.

federal matter unless proven otherwise.

That problem was addressed in 1934 when the law was amended so the bureau could move if the case had not been broken within seven days. Under the amendment, the presumption was that the victim had been moved across state lines by that time. The presumptive period was shortened to 24 hours after the 1956 kidnaping and death of one-month-old Peter Weinberger on Long Island. As the Mann Act had done in 1910, the kidnaping law pushed forward the notion that some crimes were national in scope and could be fought only through cooperative action.

However, while bureau agents could make arrests, they still did not have full police powers, and they carried guns only in special circumstances. Local police could and did help search for felons, but local forces often were filled with officers or administrators on the take. More than one desperado escaped a dragnet because of prior warning provided by a police buddy.

The kidnaping law was only a start. Another series of spectacular crimes that included the deaths of bureau agents was about to help bring about the most sweeping law changes to affect the bureau during its short history. The Kansas City Massacre

BELOW: Notorious bank robber and murderer Charles 'Pretty Boy' Floyd, prime suspect in the Kansas City Massacre of 1933.

of 1933, which featured Charles Arthur 'Pretty Boy' Floyd, was one of the more well-publicized crimes of the period.

Floyd was born in Oklahoma in 1901. He struggled through the life of a hard-scrabble Dust Bowl farmer for a number of years, but with his wife pregnant and no job in sight, he took up a gun. The list of his crimes and killing is massive. He robbed a payroll in St Louis, got caught and spent three years in jail. After he got out, he killed the man who shot his father. Once again a hunted man, Floyd moved on to Kansas City, where he acquired his nickname when a madam named Ann Chambers spotted him and said, 'I want you for myself, pretty boy.' He later killed another madam's two sons, but when the press caught up with her for a couple of quotes, all she wanted to know was whether the cops had gotten 'Pretty Boy' yet.

A long string of bank robberies and murders started in 1930. After knocking over several small-town banks, Floyd was captured when the driver of his getaway car smashed into a telephone pole. He was sentenced to 15 years, but true to his vow never to go to prison again, he kicked out a train window while his guards dozed and jumped to the embankment below.

Floyd then got together with Bill 'The Killer' Miller and knocked over a string of Michigan banks. They returned to Kansas City, shot two men dead, and then hit some banks in Kentucky. In Bowling Green, Ohio, two police officers attempted to stop the men, and Floyd killed one of them. But the other officer killed Miller, and Floyd went into hiding, eventually returning to Kansas City.

On 21 July 1931, Prohibition agents broke into his hiding place and bullets flew. Floyd shot agent Curtis C Burks in the head, killing him, and then escaped. With nowhere else to run, Floyd returned home to the Cookson Hills, joined up with a former preacher, and started a new series of bank robberies, including two in one day. It was said that some of his hometown people, who saw him as something of a Robin Hood, wished him luck when they spotted him strolling in to take another bank.

Then came the Kansas City Massacre, the hit that mortified the public and truly earned Floyd, whether or not he was involved, his permanent spot in villainy. On 17 June 1933, Bureau of Investigation Agent Raymond Caffrey, Police Chief Otto Reed of McAlester, Oklahoma, two Kansas City detectives and three other bureau agents were transferring Frank Nash, an escapee who had eluded police for three years, from a

RIGHT: Adam Richetti, captured in an Ohio gun battle in 1934, was sentenced to death for his role in the Kansas City Massacre.

BELOW: The corncrib near East Liverpool, Ohio, where federal agents shot and killed Pretty Boy Floyd in October 1934.

train to a car for the final leg of a trip to Leavenworth. All men were armed. As the men were getting into the car, three other men stepped up and started firing machine guns and pistols. The detectives, Reed and Caffrey were killed and two other bureau agents were wounded. Nash also died. Caffrey had been with the bureau for five years and was 31 years old.

Questions remain about the identity of the killers and their purpose. Some thought they were attempting to rescue Nash and killed him by mistake. Others argue that Nash simply knew too much about the underworld and had become expendable. The bureau, based on witness accounts, decided that gun-for-hire Vern Miller, Adam Richetti and Floyd were the killers.

Miller was found several months later, tortured and beaten to death in gangland style. Richetti was captured following a gun battle in 1934 and was executed after being convicted of murder. Floyd met his final reckoning in an Ohio farm field. Shortly after the massacre, Floyd had written Kansas

City police to protest his innocence, but the police were not convinced, not surprising considering Floyd's past. Surrounded by a dragnet on 22 October 1934, Floyd tried to escape across a field. Bureau agents and local police cut him down. Agent Melvin Purvis, who just a couple of months earlier had been involved in the final shootout with John Dillinger, ran to Floyd as he lay dying and confirmed the man's identity. He also asked him about the massacre. 'I didn't do it,' Floyd is said to have replied. 'I wasn't in on it.'

The Floyd episode was only one of several in which the best-known gangsters would die in blazing gun battles. The bureau would emerge from the period with a high public profile. Never again, for good or for bad, would it languish in obscurity. In 1935, its name was changed to the Federal Bureau of Investigation.

Stunned and appalled by the lawlessness that seemed to have taken over the whole nation, citizens and politicians alike looked for the quick cure. One suggested prescrip-

BELOW: Authorities view the body of Pretty Boy Floyd in an Ohio morgue shortly after his shooting.

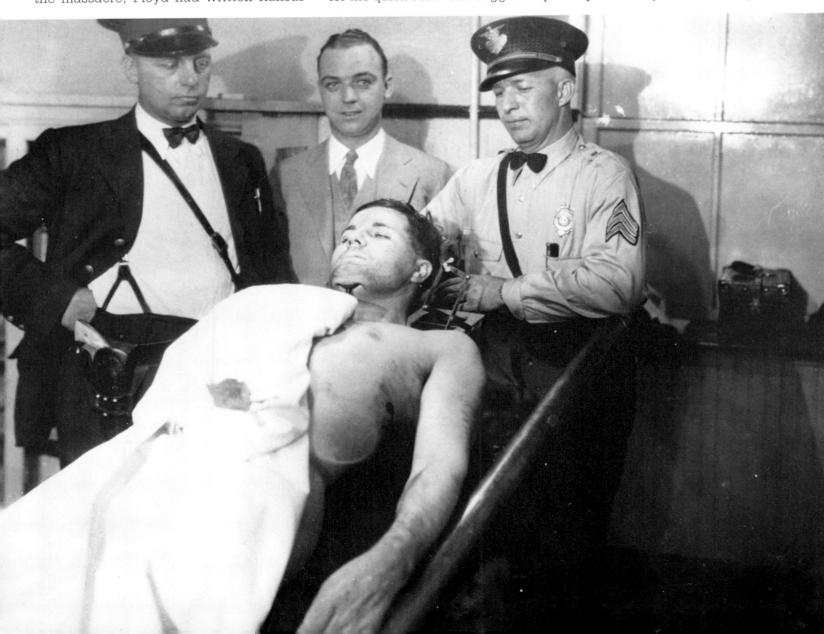

tion was a proposal to turn all police power over to the federal government. That move would certainly have created the long-dreaded police state, and such people as Attorney General Homer Cummings also quickly recognized it was politically unworkable. An organization big enough to attempt to fight every crime in every hamlet would have been massive indeed.

Cummings had another plan, one that would bolster the public's respect for lawmen and thereby get the average citizen involved in the fight against crime. Meanwhile, Cummings would introduce new federal laws that would allow Federal Bureau of Investigation agents to go after the big name 'public enemies.' The plan was effective as far as it went. But it created a tendency for the public and for J Edgar Hoover to focus on the 'big hit' and to ignore underlying causes and major organizations, such as the Mafia, that were building their power.

President Franklin Delano Roosevelt signed several important acts into law in May and June of 1934. The first law made the killing or assault of a federal officer a federal crime. Before this, the federal

government had no jurisdiction. Another law made it a federal crime to extort anything of value involving interstate commerce. The Lindbergh Kidnap Law was amended to include cases where no ransom was demanded, and to allow the FBI to enter a case after a seven-day waiting period. The Fugitive Felon Act made it a federal crime to cross state lines to avoid prosecution or to dodge giving testimony in certain types of cases. As a partial approach to the problem of corruption among federal employees taking care of prisons, a law made it a federal crime to aid in or to conspire to aid in the escape of a prisoner from a federal prison.

The National Bank Act was broadened to allow the FBI to act on any robbery of a bank organized or operating under the umbrella of federal rules. Another law made it illegal to transport stolen property worth $5000 or more across state lines. Stolen property, of course, includes cars and it was under this statute that the FBI first went after John Dillinger. (In the future, critics would accuse the FBI of focusing on stolen cars as a way to bolster its crime-solving figures.) The Federal Anti-Racketeering Act made it ille-

gal to interfere with interstate commerce through violence, intimidation or threats. And the National Firearms Act gave the FBI secondary jurisdiction over firearms violations. Finally, FBI agents were given full police powers and the right to carry firearms. at all times while on duty.

Roosevelt sounded the call to the public at the signing ceremony:

I regard this action today as an event of the first importance. So far as the federal government is concerned, there will be no relenting. But there is one thing more. Law enforcement and gangster extermination cannot be made completely effective so long as a substantial part of the public looks with tolerance upon known criminals, permits public officials to be corrupted or intimidated by them or applauds efforts to romanticize crime.

Federal men are constantly facing machine gun fire in the persuit of gangsters. I ask citizens, individually and in organized groups, to recognize the facts and meet them with courage and determination.

I stand squarely behind the efforts of

the Department of Justice to bring to book every lawbreaker, big and little.

Cummings was the point man, the one out in front of these efforts at the time. But Hoover was learning about public relations from Cummings. Hoover would be the one in the headlines soon and he quickly realized that the way to stay there was to trumpet the big catches, even if he had to play with the facts of the case occasionally. Later in life, when he attempted to emphasize the scientific, forensic achievements of his organization, he discovered it simply didn't play on Main Street America.

But the new FBI and its new laws were about to shatter the popular gangster in a blaze of blood and bullets. Within the next few months, agents would gun down John Dillinger, 'Baby Face' Nelson and Ma Barker and her boys. Even today, many Americans think of this period of the bureau's history when they talk about the FBI.

John Herbert Dillinger; it was a name that J Edgar Hoover despised more than most, and no one was really certain why. True, Dillinger robbed numerous banks and businesses, escaped from jail at least twice and may have killed once. Perhaps it was the attention he received. Newspapers of the time gleefully recounted his every exploit without so much as a question about his conduct. He achieved the sort of dubious hero status that the government was trying to discourage.

John Dillinger was born in Indianapolis, Indiana in 1903. He made decent grades in school and apparently was a gifted athlete. But after his father moved the family to a farm in Mooresville, Indiana, when Dillinger was a teenager, he started getting in trouble. In 1923, he stole a car. Scared that he would go to jail, he ran and joined the Navy to get away from the area. That lasted only a short time and after deserting, he returned home and got married.

But by September 1924, he was in trouble again. He and a buddy jumped a grocer in an attempt to steal the day's receipts. The robbery failed, but Dillinger went to prison for what would be nine years after he was persuaded to throw himself at the mercy of the court. His partner in the attempted robbery served about two years. While in prison, Dillinger attempted to escape at least five times, all of them unsuccessful. Also while in prison, Dillinger met Harry Pierpont, John Hamilton, Russell Clark and Charles Makley, the core of the group that would later rob many banks.

Dillinger was paroled in May 1933, leaving with a list of places to rob so he could finance a massive prison break of his future bank-busting buddies. He quickly went to work with a handful of other men and soon had robbed a string of businesses and banks. Wearing a straw boater and leaping gracefully over bank railings, he earned his reputation as the gentlemanly bank robber.

After robbing several banks, Dillinger finally had enough money. He bribed a foreman at a thread-making company in Chicago to secrete several guns inside a barrel headed for the shirt factory at the Michigan City, Indiana, prison where his buddies were incarcerated. Meanwhile, Dillinger returned to Dayton, Ohio, to see his new girlfriend, and was promptly captured at her apartment. While Dillinger was sitting in jail, Pierpont and nine other men broke out of prison using the guns Dillinger sent. A couple of weeks later, Pierpont, Makley, Clark, Hamilton and Edward Shouse walked into the Lima, Ohio, jail,

identified themselves as police officers, and asked to see Dillinger. But when Sheriff Jess Sarber asked to see credentials, Pierpont pulled a gun. Sarber moved for his weapon and Pierpont shot him twice. Dillinger was free again. Sarber died.

Eight days later the gang hit the Peru, Indiana, police arsenal. Disguised as tourists, Pierpont and Dillinger asked police on duty what they had planned in case the Dillinger gang came to town. The cops proudly showed their weapons, and Dillinger and Pierpont just as proudly relieved them of shotguns, machine guns, pistols, rifles, bullet-proof vests and bags of ammunition.

The gang, after careful planning, robbed the Central National Bank in Greencastle, Indiana, and made off with a huge haul of more than $75,000 in cash and bonds. A month later, Dillinger narrowly escaped a

OPPOSITE: John Dillinger, posing with a Colt .38 in one hand and a submachine gun in the other, shortly before his death.

BELOW: Mooresville, Indiana, Dillinger's home town.

ABOVE: Despite this armed guard outside the Crown Point, Indiana, jail, John Dillinger was able to pull off one of the most sensational jailbreaks in history on 3 March 1934.

inger always denied it.

Tucson was bad news for the Dillinger gang, but good news for the forces of law and order. The whole gang was rounded up after Clark and Makley were caught following a fire at their hotel. Firemen thought one of their suitcases was rather heavy, and when they opened it they found it stuffed with weapons.

Dillinger was taken to the Crown Point, Indiana, 'escape-proof' jail to await trial on robberies and for the murder of O'Malley. He was about to write another chapter in his already colorful history. While in jail, Dillinger obtained a razor and carved a handgun from a piece of wood. He colored the gun with bootblack and on 3 March 1934, pulled it on his jailers. Later, a self-satisfied grin on his face, Dillinger would be photographed holding the fake weapon. Dillinger stole Sheriff Lillian Holley's car and drove across the state line into rural Indiana. Although he would escape from at least a couple of more police traps, he was on the road to his final destination. FBI agents, at the request of local police, had sought Dillinger before. But when he took Holley's car across state lines, he violated a federal law and became Hoover's pet project.

Dillinger moved his headquarters to St Paul, Minnesota, and it didn't take long to put together a new gang. Among those who joined him was the maniacal killer Lester Gillis, better known as Baby Face Nelson. The first hit came at the Security National Bank and Trust Company in Sioux Falls, South Dakota, just three days after Dillinger's escape. Nelson killed one police officer. Meanwhile, hundreds of Sioux Falls citizens watched as the gang lined up practically the whole police force outside the bank. The citizens thought they were watching the filming of a movie. In one of the clever ruses that had become a trademark of Dillinger robberies, one of his gang members had come to town the day before and convinced people that he was preparing to film a gangster movie there.

Several days later, a robbery in Mason City, Iowa, went awry and Dillinger and another gang member were wounded. While he was recovering from those wounds, the FBI first caught up with him at an apartment in St Paul on 31 March 1934. Two FBI agents knocked on the apartment door and Dillinger's girlfriend, Billie Frechette, answered. She stalled for a moment, and then one of the agents was distracted by another gang member coming up the stairs. One agent followed that man out on a ruse, and Dillinger and Frechette fled out the back, spraying bullets to deter pursuit.

trap at a doctor's office. That near-capture ended with Dillinger wheeling his car onto a side street after a high-speed, side-by-side chase down Chicago's streets. Dillinger's luck and reputation were still holding.

The gang moved to Wisconsin and, while robbing a Racine bank, were nearly captured. They got away this time by taking hostages, both of whom were released unharmed. They took a vacation in Florida and then, on the way to Tucson, Arizona, allegedly robbed the First National Bank of Chicago, during which police officer Patrick O'Malley was killed. Police fingered Dillinger and Hamilton as the killers, but Dill-

One of the agents, however, got off a shot that hit Dillinger in the leg.

The gang decided things were too hot in St Paul, so they retired to a rural Wisconsin resort known as Little Bohemia. It was to be the scene of another harrowing escape, and one of immense embarrassment for the FBI. Special Agent Melvin Purvis, head of the FBI office in Chicago (and the ranking bureau man on the scene when Pretty Boy Floyd was shot) got a tip that Dillinger and his deadly buddies were at Little Bohemia. He moved dozens of agents to the area on 22 April 1934.

As the agents moved in, three customers walked out and got in a car. After ordering them to stop, the agents fired, killing one man and wounding another. The gangsters they were after went out the back door and a gun battle ensued. Mostly, though, the agents were firing at a lodge empty of anyone but the gangsters' girlfriends. Years later, bullet holes in the walls of the lodge remained preserved.

The Little Bohemia fiasco had one positive side to it in that President Roosevelt

ABOVE: John Dillinger, second from right, back at the Crown Point jail in January 1934 after his capture in Arizona.

LEFT: Evelyn 'Billie' Frechette, Dillinger's sweetheart, speaking with her attorney at her trial for harboring Dillinger.

was able to use it as ammunition in pushing through his massive crime control package. But it also served as more fodder for the media, which was reporting on Dillinger as if he were a movie star. *Time* magazine turned his exploits, starting with the Crown Point jail break, into a graphic that resembled a board game, including skulls at the places people were killed. The same issue of the magazine compared him with Tom Sawyer and speculated that in younger days he may have dreamed of being another Abraham Lincoln or Jesse James. Numerous people no doubt saw him simply as someone who had taken money from bankers who had grown rich by robbing the poor. There is ample evidence that Dillinger was enjoying all the publicity.

All the hype about the man who time and time again had duped the law helped seal Dillinger's fate. Hoover told agents to take him alive if possible, but Attorney General Homer Cummings simply told them to shoot to kill. Hoover put out a $10,000 reward and another $10,000 was put up by five states where he had robbed banks.

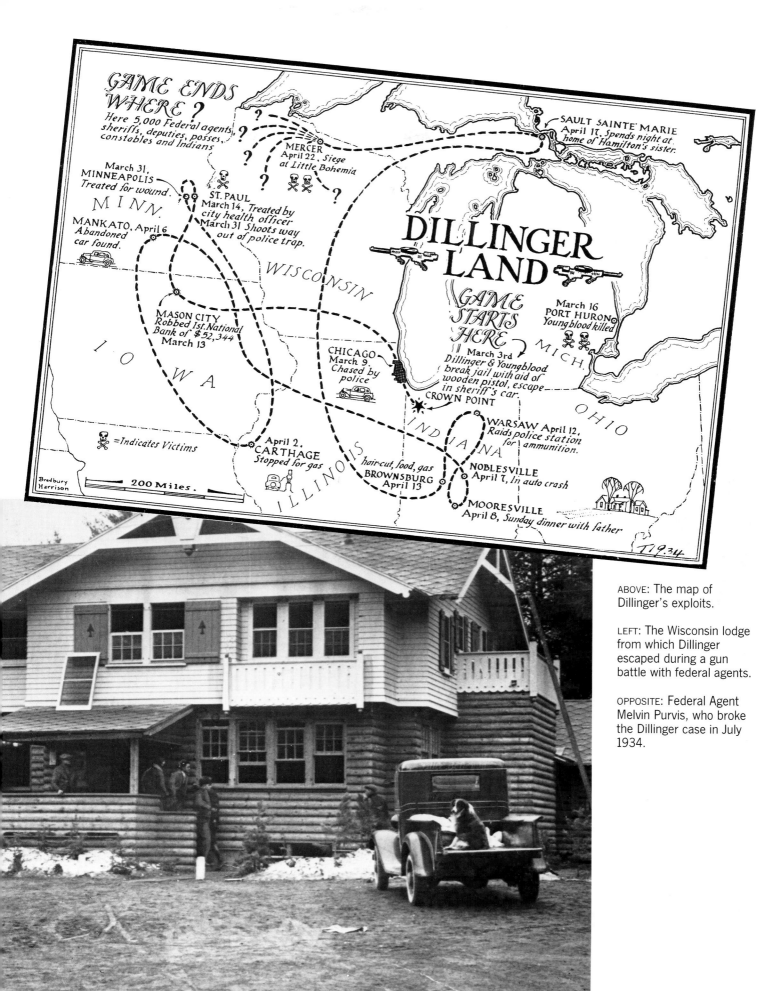

GAME ENDS WHERE? Here 5,000 Federal agents, sheriffs, deputies, posses, constables and Indians

SAULT SAINTE MARIE April 17, Spends night at home of Hamilton's sister.

MERCER April 22, Siege at Little Bohemia

March 31, **MINNEAPOLIS** Treated for wound.

MANKATO, April 6 Abandoned car found.

ST. PAUL March 14, Treated by city health officer March 31 Shoots way out of police trap.

MINN.

WISCONSIN

DILLINGER LAND

GAME STARTS HERE

March 16 **PORT HURON** Youngblood killed

MASON CITY Robbed 1st.National Bank of $52,344 March 13

IOWA

CHICAGO March 9, Chased by police

March 3rd Dillinger & Youngblood break jail with aid of wooden pistol, escape in sheriff's car. **CROWN POINT**

MICH.

OHIO

INDIANA

WARSAW April 12, Raids police station for ammunition.

= Indicates Victims

April 2, **CARTHAGE** Stopped for gas

ILLINOIS

hair-cut, food, gas **BROWNSBURG** April 13

NOBLESVILLE April 7, In auto crash

MOORESVILLE April 8, Sunday dinner with father

Bradbury Harrison

200 Miles.

T.9.34

ABOVE: The map of Dillinger's exploits.

LEFT: The Wisconsin lodge from which Dillinger escaped during a gun battle with federal agents.

OPPOSITE: Federal Agent Melvin Purvis, who broke the Dillinger case in July 1934.

The final break on the Dillinger case was a matter of luck. Anna Sage, popularly known as 'The Woman in Red,' was looking for a deal. The federal government wanted to deport her to Rumania as an undesirable alien. She could lead the FBI to Dillinger if they would stop the deportation proceedings. Purvis readily agreed. On 22 July 1934, Dillinger, accompanied by Sage and another woman, walked out of the Biograph Theater in Chicago after watching a movie. Sage was wearing red, as prearranged. Purvis, Special Agent Samuel P Cowley, other bureau agents and police officers from East Chicago were waiting. When he spotted Dillinger, Purvis lit a cigar to signal the others. As the agents and police moved in, Dillinger saw what was happening and started to draw a gun. He was mowed down before he could fire a shot. Dillinger was dead.

The reaction to Dillinger's death was strange and diverse. Witnesses on the scene dipped pieces of cloth in his blood. Some of the newspapers that had been immortalizing the hoodlum suddenly switched positions and hailed the death of Public Enemy Number One. Others, however, poured out their sympathy for Dillinger, Kelly, Nelson and other gangsters shot down by FBI agents during the relatively brief period in the mid-1930s when shootouts were common. Indeed, virtually every member of Dillinger's gang was either shot to death or, like Pierpont, died in the electric chair.

During the period following the death of Dillinger, citizens started hearing more public pronouncements by Hoover. He described the criminals his agents were chasing as 'scum from the boiling pot of the underworld,' 'public rats,' and 'craven beasts.' He railed against the parole system that let criminals out of prison, and he told Mom and Dad that they could help fight crime by bringing Junior up right.

Purvis' handling of the ambush of Dillinger and his subsequent killing of Pretty Boy Floyd should have earned him honors. Instead, with much of the nation's press glorifying Purvis, Hoover reworked the Dillinger shooting story and pushed Purvis out of the limelight, a habit that would continue through the years. Hoover preferred to think of the agency as a 'We' organization. Purvis quit the FBI in 1935. He went to Hollywood and became head of the 'Post Toasties Law and Order Patrol' and later was the announcer for the unsanctioned 'Top Secrets of the FBI' radio program. In 1960, he shot himself to death.

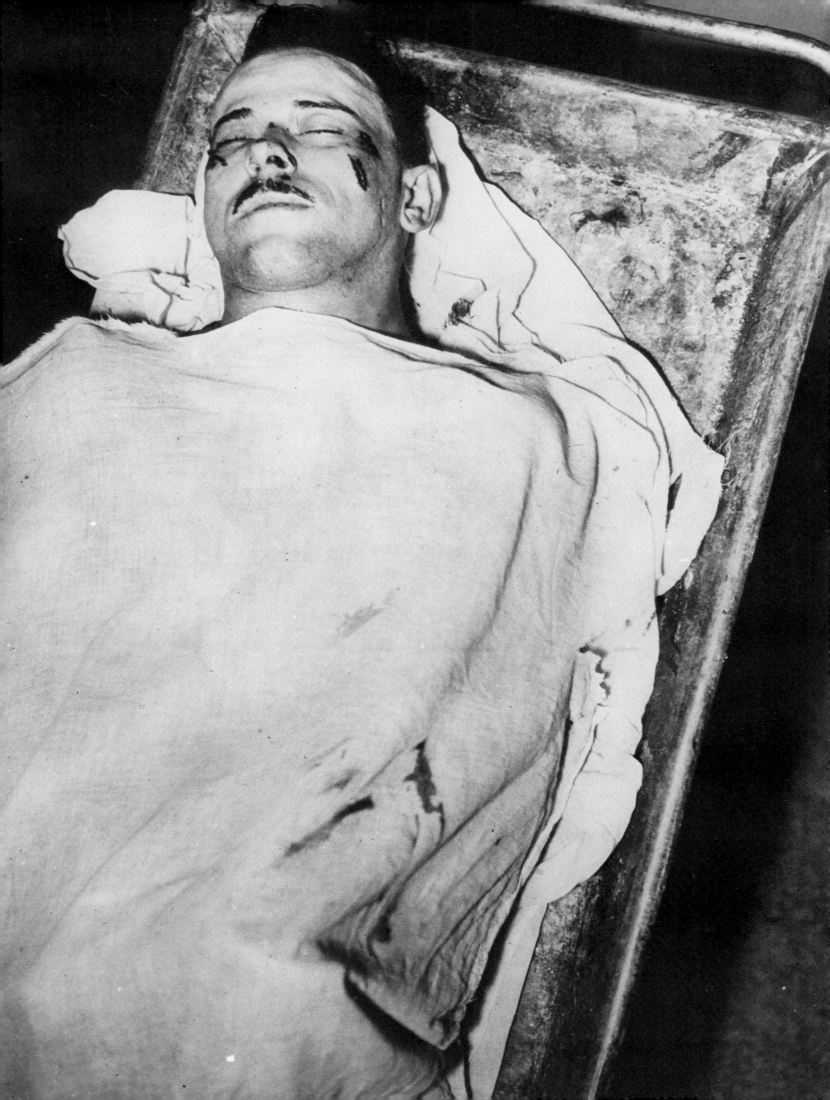

ABOVE: W Carter Baum, the federal agent killed by Baby Face Nelson in the Wisconsin shootout with Dillinger's gang.

Nelson was arrested for the robbery of a Chicago jewelry store in 1931 and served time in the penitentiary at Joliet. He escaped after less than a year, and then took to robbing small banks in Iowa, Nebraska and Wisconsin with John Paul Chase, Eddie Green and Tommy Carroll.

Nelson eventually hooked up with Homer Van Meter and John Hamilton, who ran with John Dillinger after he broke out of the Crown Point Jail using a wooden gun he carved with a razor blade. Dillinger and Van Meter didn't much care for Nelson or his crazy antics, but Nelson had already cased a couple of ripe banks. Dillinger quickly got a taste of Nelson's special brand of insanity. In March 1934, the two were riding in a car with Nelson driving when Nelson hit another car. When the driver of that car, Theodore Kidder, hopped out and started screaming, Nelson plugged him between the eyes. Dillinger, no sweet mama's boy himself, was appalled.

Nelson's first run-in with the FBI came at the Little Bohemia lodge in Wisconsin. The agents actually were after Dillinger, but he escaped quickly. Nelson remained behind spraying shots at the agents. When two agents caught up with him at a nearby resort the next morning, Nelson hopped from his stolen car and blasted away, killing Special Agent W Carter Baum. Baum had been with the FBI for four years and was 29 when he died.

Nelson skipped to California but simply could not stay away from the Midwest, where he had made his reputation. His whole gang, with the exception of his wife and Chase, was dead by that time, so Nelson really just wandered around. On 27 November 1934, FBI agents Sam Cowley, who had participated in the Dillinger shooting, and Herman Hollis, caught up with the Nelsons and Chase on a country road near Fox River Grove, Illinois.

A car chase ensued, with bullets flying in both directions. Nelson finally pulled his car over and, while his wife ran into a field, Chase and Nelson hunkered down for a shootout. Construction workers nearby witnessed the wild melee. The agents and the two bandits exchanged fire from behind cover for a while, but Nelson seemed to tire of that. He stood up firing and started walking toward the agents. They hit him numerous times, but he kept coming. The scene, as described by those workers, came straight from a cheap gangster movie, with Nelson yelling for the agents to 'Come and get it.'

Nelson reached a ditch where Cowley was crouched and shot him with his

Dillinger was dead, but the FBI's war against the gangsters was not quite over. Lester Gillis, later known as George 'Baby Face' Nelson, was a diminutive man who spent most of his life trying to make up for his size. His equalizer was his machine gun and he was one of the few of the well-known gangsters who went out of his way to kill. Most hoodlums, not known to be a squeamish lot, would have nothing to do with him. By the time he died in a furious gun battle, he had taken three FBI agents, one policeman and an unknown number of other people to the grave with him.

Born in 1908 near Chicago's stockyards, Nelson grew up as a street tough. He never knew anything else. He went from petty thievery to stickups to a protection racket for businesses that didn't want him to rob them. Baby Face was too much even for Al Capone's organization. He helped line up unions that would kick back dues to Capone, but occasionally roughed someone up so much that he killed them. He was dropped from the trade.

machine gun. Cowley died the next day. Hollis emptied one gun and then drew another. Nelson hit him and killed him. Hollis had been with the FBI for seven years and was 31 when he died. Cowley, who at the time was one of Hoover's most trusted agents, was 35 and had been an agent for five years. But Nelson had been mortally wounded. When his naked body, stripped to try to avoid identification, was found in a ditch the next day, it was riddled with 17 bullets. Chase was caught in California a month after the shootout and was sentenced to life in prison. Nelson's wife served one year and then disappeared.

Hoover would say later that during the two-year period in which his agents were fighting the criminals who fit the gangster mold of the day, eight gangsters were killed and the FBI lost four agents. Nelson killed three of those men. But on that November day when Baby Face and two FBI agents died, bureau men still had one of the wildest shootouts ahead of them.

The Barker gang was a real oddity in the gangster era. Arizona Donnie Clark 'Ma' Barker was the brains behind the organiza-

LEFT: The wanted poster for Lester M Gillis, alias Baby Face Nelson.

BELOW: Local police in Illinois examine Nelson's body after he was killed in a shootout with federal agents.

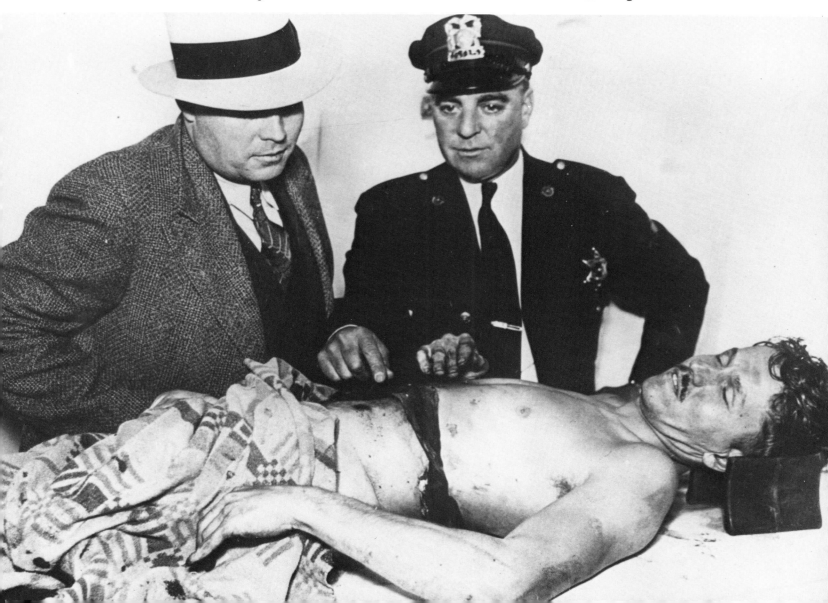

tion, but her sons carried out the crimes. She was never formally charged with anything. Born in Missouri, Ma Barker was the stereotypical overprotective mother to her four boys, Arthur ('Doc'), Fred, Herman and Lloyd. When they started getting in trouble at a young age, she was always there to raise hell until the boys were released from jail. Eventually they graduated to bigger and bloodier things. Herman's career was shorter than the rest. After escaping custody on a bank robbery charge in 1927, he and another man were caught in a gun battle in which Kansas City police officer J E Marshall was killed. He escaped that one, but when he was trapped again a short time later he shot himself in the head. Herman was the oldest boy and, at age 14, had been the first to get in trouble.

The others weren't far behind. Doc and Freddie probably were the worst, never hesitating to kill when they thought it necessary. Doc killed a night watchman while trying to steal a shipment of drugs in 1918. He spent the next 13 years in prison. Freddie went to prison for robbing a bank in 1926 and was not released until 1931. Lloyd robbed a post office in 1922 and was sen-

TOP: 'Ma' Barker, who guided her four sons into careers of crime.

ABOVE: Alvin Karpis, a member of the Barker gang, captured by the FBI in May 1936.

tenced to 25 years. He served the full amount, and therefore was the only brother never to join the gang. Still, his death was violent. His wife shot him in 1949. Hoover once said that the jailing of her boys turned Ma Barker into a 'veritable beast of prey.' He seemed to be right. By the time Doc and Freddie got out of prison in the early 1930s, they had learned new criminal skills. Freddie brought with him Alvin 'Old Creepy' Karpis, to whom Ma took an immediate liking and began to treat as her own son.

It would be difficult to list all the crimes committed by the Barkers, and they didn't all work together all the time. Freddie and Karpis killed the police chief in Pocaholtas, Arkansas, in November 1931. Earlier, they had killed a sheriff in Missouri. Freddie, Doc and Karpis killed two policemen and wounded a civilian while robbing a Minnesota bank in 1932, killed a policeman while robbing a payroll in 1933, and then Freddie and Doc killed another policeman while robbing a Federal Reserve mail truck. They also disposed of Ma's boyfriend after they tired of him, and later killed a doctor who botched operations to change their facial features and fingerprints. In between the killings,

they pulled off numerous robberies, usually getting away with large sums. The largest came from the Cloud County Bank in Concordia, Kansas, where the take was $250,000.

Then the gang tried kidnaping. They picked up $100,000 for the abduction of St Paul brewer William A Hamm Jr in 1933, and then made $200,000 on the kidnaping of Minneapolis banker Edward G Bremer. But Doc Barker left a fingerprint at the scene of that crime and suddenly the Barker gang was in the headlines. Doc was traced by the FBI to Chicago and Melvin Purvis, the agent who shot Pretty Boy Floyd and engineered the shooting of John Dillinger, took him on the street without a fight. Doc had left his gun at his hiding place. He was sent to Alcatraz, the new super prison for super crooks, and in 1939 was killed by guards as he attempted to escape.

The FBI found a map of Florida in Doc's apartment and using that, they traced Ma and Freddie to Oklawaha on 16 January 1935. They ordered the Barkers out of their cottage. Ma and Freddie replied with gun fire. Forty-five minutes later, the FBI agents had cut the cottage to shreds and Ma and

BELOW LEFT: Arthur 'Doc' Barker (left) was captured by federal agents in Chicago and returned to St Paul to face kidnap charges. His mother and brother were traced to Florida, where agents gunned them down.

BELOW: An editorial cartoon shows J Edgar Hoover taking criminals to Alcatraz. Doc Barker was sent there, and was killed when he tried to escape.

SONG HIT OF THE YEAR

I'M PUTTING ALL MY YEGGS IN ONE BASKET—

G-MAN HOOVER

ALCATRAZ ISLAND PRISON

Best o' Luck to J Edgar Hoover

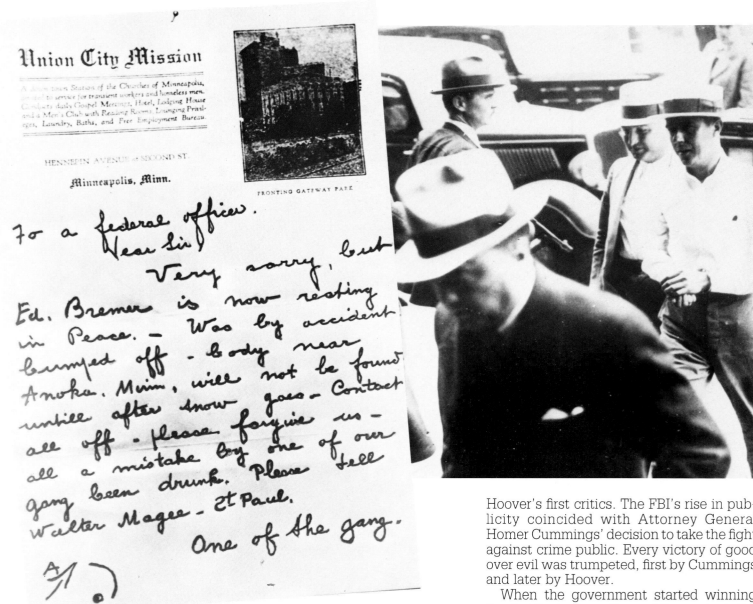

Union City Mission

A down town Station of the Churches of Minneapolis,
devoted to service for transient workers and homeless men.
Conducts daily Gospel Meetings, Hotel, Lodging House
and a Men's Club with Reading Rooms, Lounging Privileges, Laundry, Baths, and Free Employment Bureau.

HENNEPIN AVENUE at SECOND ST.

Minneapolis, Minn.

FRONTING GATEWAY PARK

To a federal officer.
Dear Sir)
     Very sorry, but
Ed. Bremer is now resting
in Peace. — Was by accident
bumped off - body near
Anoka. Minn, will not be found
untill after snow goes - Contact
all off - please forgive us -
all a mistake by one of our
gang been drunk. Please tell
Walter Magee - St Paul.
          One of the gang.

TOP RIGHT: J Edgar Hoover
(left) leads Alvin Karpis
into the Federal Building
in St Paul. Hoover was
also in on the highly-
publicized bust in New
Orleans.

TOP LEFT: A letter from the
1933 abduction of St Paul
banker Edward Bremer.

Freddie were dead. Freddie was hit 11 times and Ma three. It is believed that Ma actually committed suicide.

More than a year later, Karpis would be arrested in New Orleans, with J Edgar Hoover in on the bust after critics had attacked him for never having made an arrest himself. Karpis pleaded guilty to his crimes and spent the next 33 years in prison. He was deported to Canada on his release in 1969. Hoover considered Karpis the last of the big-time, freelance gangsters and with his arrest, following a massive manhunt, came the close of an era. Much of the major crime was moving underground, and it would be 25 years before the FBI would address the modern descendants of the gangsters: the Mafia.

By the time the gangsters were gone, the FBI in general, and J Edgar Hoover in particular, had moved from obscurity to fame. They had become true American heroes. But that attention also brought out some of

Hoover's first critics. The FBI's rise in publicity coincided with Attorney General Homer Cummings' decision to take the fight against crime public. Every victory of good over evil was trumpeted, first by Cummings and later by Hoover.

When the government started winning the battle to turn the public against the gangsters, Hollywood followed, in no small part prompted by the censor's scissors. Censorship increased as violence on the screen increased. The Legion of Decency was formed and censors started enforcing the long-dormant Film Production Code. Violence from the movie *Scarface* (1932) was cut, and censors forced the producer to change the ending to show more respect for law enforcement. Instead of being shot down in the street, the gangster in the movie is tried and sentenced to hang. Machine guns weren't allowed in the movies, and any form of disrespect for the police was taboo.

By 1935, the moviemakers were evading the censor's scissors by turning the scripts around. The G-Man became the hero and the hoodlums took their turn as the bad guys. *G-Men,* released in 1935 and starring James Cagney as the special agent, may have boosted the image of Hoover and the FBI more than anything before or since. It

LEFT: Hoover and Homer Cummings look over a print of the 1938 film *Crime Does Not Pay*.

BELOW: A scene from the 1932 gangster film *Scarface*, which was censored to show more respect for law enforcement.

SPIRIT OF '36 SPELLS DOOM FOR RACKETEERS

was the first major production of any type based, albeit loosely, on the story of the FBI.

Although frowned upon by the Department of Justice, producers of the movie advertised it as the true story of the copper's fight against the gangsters. The movie offered a little something for every gangster movie fan. In the script, three crooks, who represented John Dillinger, Pretty Boy Floyd and Machine Gun Kelly, kidnap Special Agent Brick Davis' girlfriend. The movie takes a good deal of cinematic license with a version of the Kansas City Massacre, the shootout at Little Bohemia and the killing of John Dillinger, although that scene had to be altered considerably because the movie code did not allow any film based on John Dillinger's life. The movie was promoted with anti-crime displays in theater lobbies. Promoters tried, despite the disclaimers of the Department of Justice, to make the public believe the film was sponsored by the government.

The film also included a thinly disguised J Edgar Hoover, who becomes the hero of the new gangster crusade. There was no role for Cummings. With the release of the film, Hoover was portrayed as the nation's chief gangbuster, a role he adopted with relish, writing and speaking extensively about the FBI and crime. Although Hoover was criticized over the years for promoting himself and for rewriting history to make the FBI look as good as possible, ego certainly was not the only factor involved. As mentioned before, he also discovered a new tactic – public relations – could rally the country behind the things he considered important: fighting crime and, later, ousting communists from society.

As Hoover's image rose, so did public sniping, not an unusual practice in Washington, DC, where anyone who seeks to exercise power is brought under the intense scrutiny of those who already have or want it. The bigger debate over liberty versus justice was part of the issue. But in addition to drawing fire over the possible abuse of police power, Hoover was also taking heat for claiming undue credit for the agency's exploits and over-dramatizing his and the bureau's prowess.

Senator Kenneth D McKellar, a Democrat from Tennessee, was one of the first to publicly castigate Hoover. The first attacks came during appropriations subcommittee hearings in April 1936. Senator McKellar questioned Hoover about the propriety of the heated gun battles with gangsters. He took him to task for the publicity the bureau was getting, and accused him of using federal money to hire writers.

Most infuriating to Hoover was the fact that Senator McKellar questioned the director's bravery and police skills by pointing out that Hoover had never investigated a case or made an arrest. The senator wondered aloud why Hoover was head of the FBI when he had no law enforcement background.

Following that grilling, Hoover quickly made sure he would have some arrests on his record before he faced another congressional inquiry. He started with a role in the highly publicized nabbing of Alvin 'Old Creepy' Karpis in New Orleans. The publicity machine that was taking shape within the bureau blew Hoover's role in the arrests out of proportion to show that the chief could work the field with the best of his agents. Interestingly, Hoover reacted immediately, and somewhat peevishly, to McKellar's dig about his professional background, while brushing off the complaints about the use of excessive firepower.

McKellar's accusations and Hoover's response did little to shower either man with glory. Hoover's supporters decried McKellar's remarks as unfair and praised the director for his role in the arrest of Karpis. Hoover's critics gave Senator McKellar's questions great importance and wide circulation, and described Hoover as a sniveling coward during the Karpis arrest. Whatever the truth of the matter, the episode has faded to insignificance.

Seven years after the first confrontation, McKellar actually praised Hoover and his

men for their work during World War II, citing Hoover as a man who stood for law enforcement in America. Hoover was so surprised by the senator's remarks, he turned and looked around the hearing room as if unconvinced he was the man McKellar was talking about. By then, however, there was little doubt that the publicity campaign had worked: J Edgar Hoover and his FBI had a firm grasp on the reputation of being America's detective agency.

BELOW: Senator Kenneth McKellar of Tennessee, shown during a 1936 radio broadcast, was one of Hoover's early critics.

LEFT: Hoover's office in July 1935.

OPPOSITE TOP: This 1935 editorial cartoon from the *Washington Star* shows the G-Men as guardians of public morality.

OPPOSITE BOTTOM: This graphic showed the network of FBI offices across the country during the 1930s.

CHAPTER FOUR

THE WAR AGAINST ESPIONAGE

With the advent of World War II, the powers of the FBI would be increased again. Some of the counterespionage work for which the bureau would be responsible would lead to early charges that the FBI was becoming the United States' own Gestapo. It is a charge that would be debated from that day on, and indeed that debate continues today. But the FBI also would score some major successes during World War II.

Not all would be success, though. The battle against the gangsters had briefly diverted the FBI's attention from its ongoing war against radicals from both ends of the ideological spectrum. During that time, it now appears, communists gained strength in America, and Japanese and German agents went about the business of stealing various military secrets and setting up their spy networks. Those preparations eventu-

BELOW: A 1930s May Day demonstration in New York.

ally culminated in such disasters as the bombing of Pearl Harbor and the breaking of secret military codes.

But quiet investigation of alleged subversive groups within the United States picked up again in 1936 when President Franklin Delano Roosevelt expressed concern to J Edgar Hoover about the activities of such groups. Roosevelt and Secretary of State Cordell Hull secretly authorized Hoover to coordinate intelligence-gathering operations among his agents, the State Department, the Military Intelligence Division and the Naval Intelligence Division.

In 1939, after a political battle with other federal agencies, Roosevelt went public with the announcement that the FBI had been set up as the coordinator of domestic intelligence work. The bureau also got the nod to do similar work in Central and South America. The announcement came just before Russia and Germany signed their non-aggression pact and the Nazis started to move in Europe. The year 1939 also was the setting for a strange case that raised a great cry against the tactics of the Department of Justice. In the end, the department and the FBI were exonerated of alleged Nazi-like tactics, but doubts remained.

LEFT: Secretary of State Cordell Hull authorized Hoover to coordinate domestic intelligence activities.

BELOW: Communists demonstrate on May Day 1935 in Philadelphia.

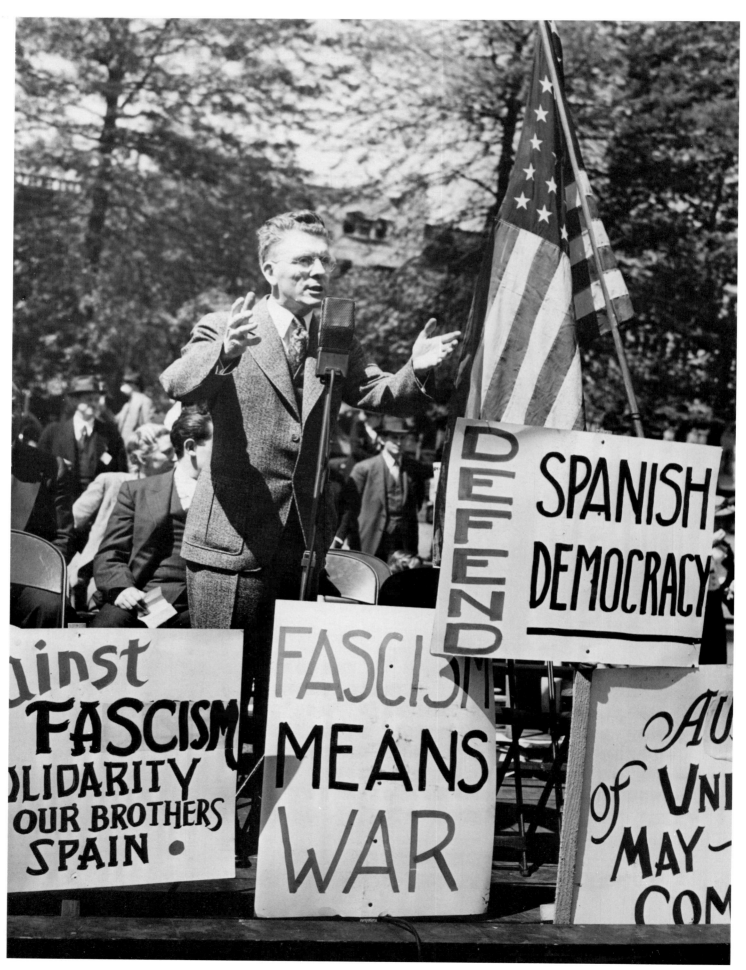

During the Spanish Civil War, federal officials started hearing rumors that the Young Communist League and others in the Detroit area were recruiting Americans to serve with the Loyalist Army in Spain. Little was done until 1939 when Hoover urged that he be given authority to investigate. Agents discovered that Phillip Raymond, a member of the Communist Party in the United States, had been recruiting, and had sent those he enlisted to fight with the Abraham Lincoln Brigade. Most of the men went by stowing away on ships or by obtaining passports under fictitious names. The FBI turned its information over to the Department of Justice.

After much waffling, the Department of Justice instructed the US District Attorney in Detroit to proceed, despite the fact that the war in Spain was over and the recruitment had ended. A grand jury returned secret indictments against about a dozen people in early 1940. FBI agents swung into action, rounding up the suspects at five AM. Hoover knew the arrests would cause an uproar, so he instructed agents to be meticulous about their treatment of the suspects. They also were advised not to mention communism in connection with the arrests.

The storm broke as expected. Communist organizations were among the strongest critics, but mainstream newspapers also editorialized against the fact that the suspects were arrested 10 hours before a federal judge would be available for arraignment, and that they were photographed handcuffed and chained together. *New Republic* magazine weighed in by comparing the FBI to the Gestapo.

The arrests had been ordered by Attorney General Frank Murphy, but when Robert H Jackson took Murphy's job in the middle of the case, he ordered the prosecution suspended. 'I can see no good to come from reviving in America at this late date the animosities of the Spanish conflict so long as the struggle has ended and some degree of amnesty at least is being extended in Spain,' Jackson said.

Jackson was admitting that he thought a mistake had been made in pressing the cases. And when Senator George W Norris called for investigation of the FBI's tactics in the matter, Jackson obliged by sending out the department's Civil Liberties Unit. Unit investigators cleared the FBI of any wrongdoing, a verdict that didn't mollify any of the bureau's critics. Some called for Hoover to be fired or for elimination of the FBI entirely, a demand that had been heard before. The demand was noted and subsequently rejected on Capitol Hill.

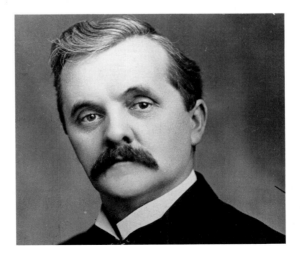

ABOVE: American communists picketed the German embassy in Washington in 1934 to protest Nazi activities.

LEFT: Attorney General Robert Jackson in 1941.

BOTTOM LEFT: Senator George Norris, an FBI critic.

OPPOSITE: Rep. Henry Teigan of Minnesota denounces Spanish fascists during a May Day rally in Washington.

ABOVE: J Edgar Hoover addresses the American Legion in Boston just before World War II.

Hoover, meanwhile, was preparing for war. He was determined the bureau would avoid some of the monstrous mistakes made during World War I. And in most ways, he succeeded. Words were part of his battle plan:

In the wave of patriotism which, fortunately, is rising throughout the nation, are the dangers of overzealousness. We must not stoop to un-American methods, no matter how great the provocation or how patriotic the aim. We should regard vigilantes or vigilante methods as abhorrent. . . . This is no time for hysteria, wild rumors, or hair-trigger prejudices. If a neighbor does not agree with your war views he isn't necessarily an enemy of America. The real spy is extremely careful about voicing opinions. . . . The citizen should consider his particular task to be fulfilled when he reports his suspicions to the nearest FBI office.

J Edgar Hoover was displaying his long memory when he wrote that salvo in the *American Magazine* in 1940. Hysterical fear about aliens was spreading through the country again, and some Americans were showing a shortened indulgence for opinions outside the mainstream. He was determined not to watch a repeat of World War I, when zealots threatened, beat or illegally arrested anyone who did not meet their personal patriotic standards.

In 1940 the American Legion proposed organizing its own investigative agency to help battle subversion. A couple of members at each Legion post would be issued badges, look into suspicious reports, and turn their evidence over to police. To Hoover, it sounded too much like the American Protective League of World War I. A compromise was struck. Legion post commanders would be designated to talk with FBI special agents about any possible problems, but the FBI and other law enforcement agencies would do all the investigating. The Legionnaires still went home happy.

Early in the war, before the United States had even entered it in fact, the FBI helped break up one of the largest wartime spy rings ever discovered. The original lead to the ring wasn't theirs, but the operation they set up following the lead led to the arrest and conviction of 33 people. A man

PHOTOGRAGH OF FREDERICK DUQUESNE TAKEN JULY 1, 1940, BY FBI AGENTS.

PHOTOGRAPH OF FREDERICK DUQUESNE IN EARLIER DAYS FOUND IN HIS POSSESSION WHEN HE WAS ARRESTED JUNE 28, 1941.

FREDERICK DUQUESNE AND WILLIAM SEBOLD, TAKEN BY FBI AGENTS MAY 29, 1940.

FREDERICK DUQUESNE, TAKEN MAY 29, 1940, BY FBI AGENTS

ABOVE: FBI photos of Frederick 'Fritz' Duquesne, the celebrated German spy.

named William Sebold was the key. A German native, he had left the country in 1921, did some traveling, and then settled in the United States and became a citizen in 1936. When he returned to Germany in 1939 for a visit, the Gestapo collared him and tried to force him into spying by threatening to harm his family.

Sebold agreed to the demand, but then contacted the American consulate in Cologne and proposed that he become a double agent. Upon his return to the United States, the FBI quickly set up a registered short-wave radio station on Long Island so Sebold could stay in contact with the Nazis.

They gave him a business office where he could meet with spies, who were filmed and monitored the whole time they were in the room. And agents pored over the microfilm, with codes and instructions to other spies already in the country, given to Sebold before he returned to America.

Primary among Sebold's American contacts was Frederick Joubert 'Fritz' Duquesne, a veteran German spy with a long history of suspected sabotage, murders and hair-raising escapades. He spied for the Dutch during the Boer War and probably spied for the Germans during World War I. More than once he escaped

83

FREDERICK DUQUESNE IN OFFICE OF WILLIAM G. SEBOLD, JUNE 25, 1941.
PICTURES TAKEN BY FBI AGENTS.

ABOVE: A series of FBI photos, taken on 25 June 1941, showing Fritz Duquesne in the office of double agent William Sebold.

death by turning double agent or fleeing. He had been an American citizen since 1913.

Sebold spent months taking instructions from the Nazis, and then sending back confusing information that had been altered but still seemed to be authentic. Anything top secret had been excised. One message told the Nazis, incorrectly of course, that American spies in Germany got information

out by engraving it on silverware and then spraying it with a metal that could be removed to reveal the message.

The Nazis apparently never suspected a thing of Sebold, even when FBI agents moved in in June 1941 and arrested 33 suspects. All pleaded guilty or were convicted in trials. The evidence was so overwhelming that one agent is reported to have said it was 'like shooting fish in a barrel.' The main fish in the case, Duquesne, was sentenced to 18 years in prison. He died in a welfare hospital in 1956.

A few days before the spy trials ended, the Japanese bombed Pearl Harbor, and the United States entered the war. The head-hunting over that disaster continues today, and the FBI has taken its lumps in many of those investigations. Hoover had, in 1940, declined to take full responsibility for monitoring possible spy activities in Hawaii. When critics assailed him, he simply pointed out that he did not have the man-power in Hawaii to keep tabs on everything.

Numerous books have been written about Pearl Harbor and it would be impossible to go through all the theories about what happened. But, from the historical perspective possible now, it seems certain that many officials, including Hoover, ignored or misinterpreted clues about the Japanese interest in Pearl Harbor. Some have even argued that Roosevelt purposely ignored the warning signs so he could use

the attack to persuade isolationists in Congress to vote for war.

Some of the misused evidence included microdots taken from a double-agent named Dusko Popov. The microdots included numerous questions about Pearl Harbor defenses that the Japanese had asked their German allies to answer. And Popov said that he told FBI agents to expect an attack on Pearl Harbor.

No matter what the complaints or suspicions about Pearl Harbor, the Federal Bureau of Investigation's record of sabotage prevention and spy hunting during World War II was exemplary. J Edgar Hoover claimed after the war that in the more than 19,000 cases of suspected sabotage his men investigated, not one was proven to be the work of an enemy of America. While it is hard to imagine that no sabotage took place, there is no question that the intelligence work of the agencies coordinated by the FBI prevented a repeat of World War I, when saboteurs went about their explosive work with abandon.

BELOW: The legal staff of the committee investigating the bombing of Pearl Harbor.

Honolulu Star-Bulletin 1st EXTRA

8 PAGES—HONOLULU, TERRITORY OF HAWAII, U. S. A., SUNDAY, DECEMBER 7, 1941—8 PAGES

★ PRICE FIVE CENTS

(Associated Press by Transpacific Telephone)

SAN FRANCISCO, Dec. 7.—President Roosevelt announced this morning that Japanese planes had attacked Manila and Pearl Harbor.

WAR!

OAHU BOMBED BY JAPANESE PLANES

SIX KNOWN DEAD, 21 INJURED, AT EMERGENCY HOSPITAL

Attack Made On Island's Defense Areas

By UNITED PRESS

WASHINGTON, Dec. 7.—Text of a White House announcement detailing the attack on the Hawaiian islands is:

"The Japanese attacked Pearl Harbor from the air and all naval and military activities on the island of Oahu, principal American base in the Hawaiian islands."

Oahu was attacked at 7:55 this morning by Japanese planes.

The Rising Sun, emblem of Japan, was seen on plane wing tips.

Wave after wave of bombers streamed through the clouded morning sky from the southwest and flung their missiles on a city resting in peaceful Sabbath calm.

According to an unconfirmed report received at the governor's office, the Japanese force that attacked Oahu reached island waters aboard two small airplane carriers.

It was also reported that at the governor's office either an attempt had been made to bomb the USS Lexington, or that it had been bombed.

CITY IN UPROAR

Within 10 minutes the city was in an uproar. As bombs fell in many parts of the city, and in defense areas the defenders of the islands went into quick action.

Army intelligence officers at Ft. Shafter announced officially shortly after 9 a. m. the fact of the bombardment by an enemy but long previous army and navy had taken immediate measures in defense.

"Oahu is under a sporadic air raid," the announcement said.

"Civilians are ordered to stay off the streets until further notice."

CIVILIANS ORDERED OFF STREETS

The army has ordered that all civilians stay off the streets and highways and not use telephones.

Evidence that the Japanese attack has registered some hits was shown by three billowing pillars of smoke in the Pearl Harbor and Hickam field area.

All navy personnel and civilian defense workers, with the exception of women, have been ordered to duty at Pearl Harbor.

The Pearl Harbor highway was immediately a mass of racing cars.

A trickling stream of injured people began pouring into the city emergency hospital a few minutes after the bombardment started.

Thousands of telephone calls almost swamped the Mutual Telephone Co., which put extra operators on duty.

At The Star-Bulletin office the phone calls deluged the single operator and it was impossible for this newspaper, for sometime, to handle the flood of calls. Here also an emergency operator was called.

HOUR OF ATTACK—7:55 A. M.

An official army report from department headquarters, made public shortly before 11, is that the first attack was at 7:55 a. m.

Witnesses said they saw at least 50 airplanes over Pearl Harbor.

The attack centered in the Pearl Harbor.

Army authorities said:

"The rising sun was seen on the wing tips of the airplanes.

Although martial law has not been declared officially, the city of Honolulu was operating under M-Day conditions.

It is reliably reported that enemy objectives under attack were Wheeler field Hickam field, Kaneohe bay and naval air station and Pearl Harbor.

Some enemy planes were reported shot down.

The body of the pilot was seen in a plane burning at Wahiawa.

Oahu appeared to be taking calmly after the first uproar of queries.

ANTIAIRCRAFT GUNS IN ACTION

First indication of the raid came shortly before 8 this morning when antiaircraft guns around Pearl Habor began sending up a thunderous barrage.

At the same time a vast cloud of black smoke arose from the naval base and also from Hickam field where flames could be seen.

BOMB NEAR GOVERNOR'S MANSION

Shortly before 9:30 a bomb fell near Washington Place, the residence of the governor. Governor Poindexter and Secretary Charles M. Hite were there.

It was reported that the bomb killed an unidentified Chinese man across the street in front of the Schuman Carriage Co. where windows were broken.

C. E. Daniels, a welder, found a fragment of shell or bomb at South and Queen Sts. which he brought into the City Hall. This fragment weighed about a pound.

At 10:05 a. m. today Governor Poindexter telephoned to The Star-Bulletin announcing he has declared a state of emergency for the entire territory.

He announced that Edouard L. Doty, executive secretary of the major disaster council, has been appointed director under the M-Day law's provisions.

Governor Poindexter urged all residents of Honolulu to remain off the street, and the people of the territory to remain calm.

Mr. Doty reported that all major disaster council wardens and medical units were on duty within a half hour of the time the alarm was given.

Workers employed at Pearl Harbor were ordered at 10:10 a. m. not to report at Pearl Harbor.

The mayor's major disaster council was to meet at the city hall at about 10:30 this morning.

At least two Japanese planes were reported at Hawaiian department headquarters to have been shot down.

One of the planes was shot down at Ft. Kamehameha and the other back of the Wo—

Turn to Page 2, Column 3

Hundreds See City Bombed

Hundreds of Honolulans who hurried to the top of Punchbowl soon after bombs began to fall, saw spread out before them the whole panorama of surprise attack and defense.

Far off over Pearl Harbor the white sky was pollka-dotted with anti-aircraft smoke.

Names of Dead and Injured

The day emergency hospital reported at 10:30 a.list of 6 killed and 11 injured.

The dead list will be enriched later. Born to a partial list:
Peter Lopes, 21, of Maui Camp.
Ed St., was reported at 6:30 a. m. to have died of injuries.

Cravalho, 27, 1700 Kalihi St., suffering from a mangled thigh, lacerations on the right leg and left arm.

A Portuguese girl, unidentified, 10 years old, died on arrival from a severe abdominal wound.

Another victim who died on arrival was Frances Ornellas, 22, 3709 Kanaina Ave.

Schools Closed

All schools on Oahu, both public and private, will remain closed Monday, territorial director of civilian defense, announced at 11 a. m. today. This does not apply elsewhere in the territory.

Editorial

HAWAII MEETS THE CRISIS

Honolulu and Hawaii will meet the emergency of war today as Honolulu and Hawaii have met every emergency in the past—coolly, calmly and with immediate and complete support of the officials, officers and troops who are in charge.

Governor Poindexter and the army and navy leaders have called upon public to remain calm, for civilians who have no essential business on the streets to stay off, and for every man and woman to do his duty.

That request, coupled with the measures promptly taken to meet the situation that has suddenly and terribly developed, will be needed.

Hawaii will do its part as a loyal American territory.

In this crisis, every difference of race, creed and color will be submerged in the one desire and determination to play the part that Americans always play in crisis.

BULLETIN

Additional Star-Bulletin extras today will cover the latest developments in this war move.

"All the News That's Fit to Print."

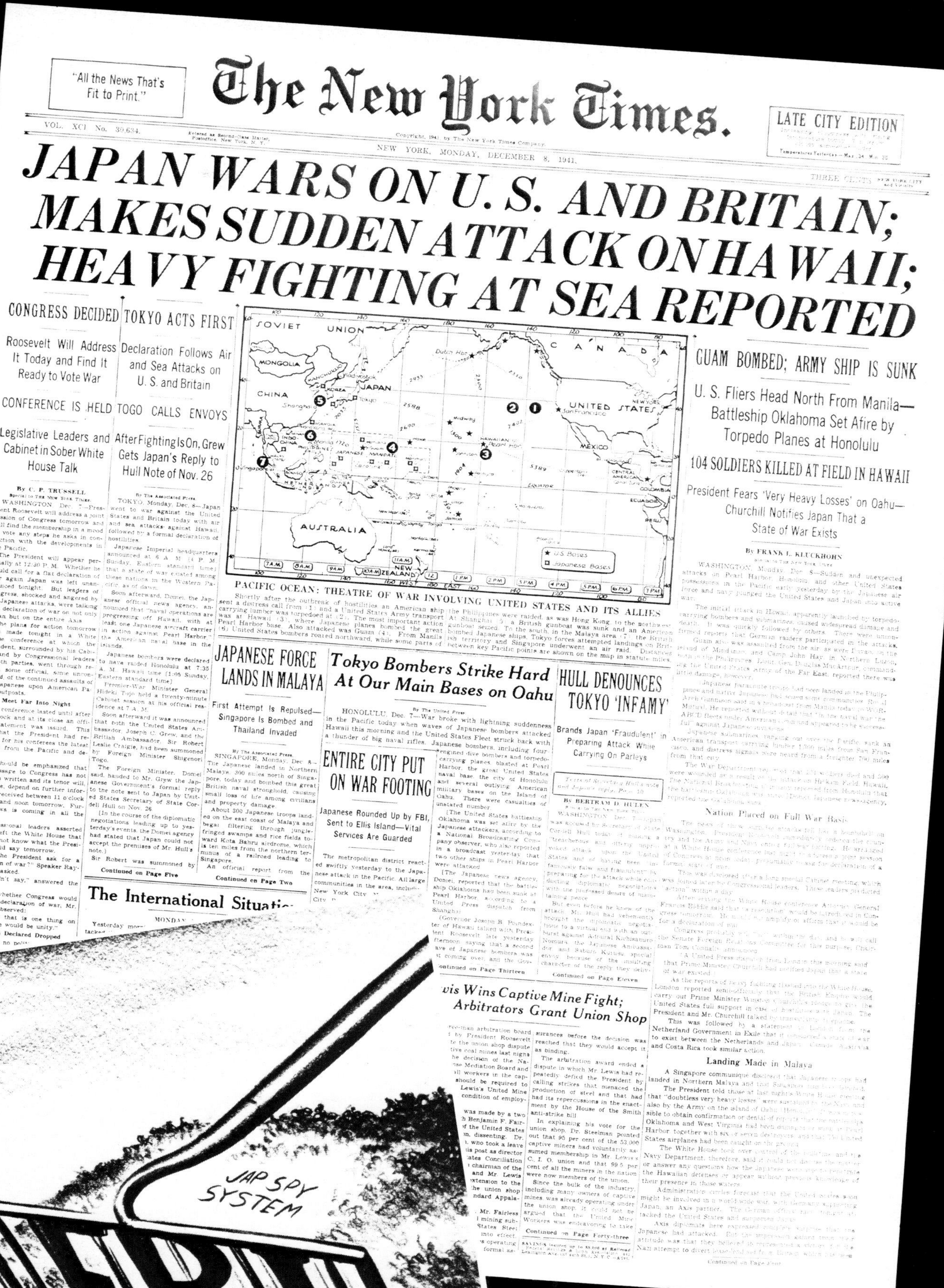

The New York Times.

LATE CITY EDITION

VOL. XCI No. 30,634. NEW YORK, MONDAY, DECEMBER 8, 1941. THREE CENTS

JAPAN WARS ON U.S. AND BRITAIN; MAKES SUDDEN ATTACK ON HAWAII; HEAVY FIGHTING AT SEA REPORTED

CONGRESS DECIDED

Roosevelt Will Address It Today and Find It Ready to Vote War

CONFERENCE IS HELD

Legislative Leaders and Cabinet in Sober White House Talk

By C. P. TRUSSELL

TOKYO ACTS FIRST

Declaration Follows Air and Sea Attacks on U.S. and Britain

TOGO CALLS ENVOYS

After Fighting Is On, Grew Gets Japan's Reply to Hull Note of Nov. 26

PACIFIC OCEAN: THEATRE OF WAR INVOLVING UNITED STATES AND ITS ALLIES

GUAM BOMBED; ARMY SHIP IS SUNK

U.S. Fliers Head North From Manila—Battleship Oklahoma Set Afire by Torpedo Planes at Honolulu

104 SOLDIERS KILLED AT FIELD IN HAWAII

President Fears 'Very Heavy Losses' on Oahu—Churchill Notifies Japan That a State of War Exists

By FRANK L. KLUCKHOHN

JAPANESE FORCE LANDS IN MALAYA

First Attempt Is Repulsed—Singapore Is Bombed and Thailand Invaded

Tokyo Bombers Strike Hard At Our Main Bases on Oahu

HULL DENOUNCES TOKYO 'INFAMY'

Brands Japan 'Fraudulent' in Preparing Attack While Carrying On Parleys

By BERTRAM D. HULEN

ENTIRE CITY PUT ON WAR FOOTING

Japanese Rounded Up by FBI, Sent to Ellis Island—Vital Services Are Guarded

The International Situation

Nation Placed on Full War Basis

Landing Made in Malaya

...vis Wins Captive Mine Fight; Arbitrators Grant Union Shop

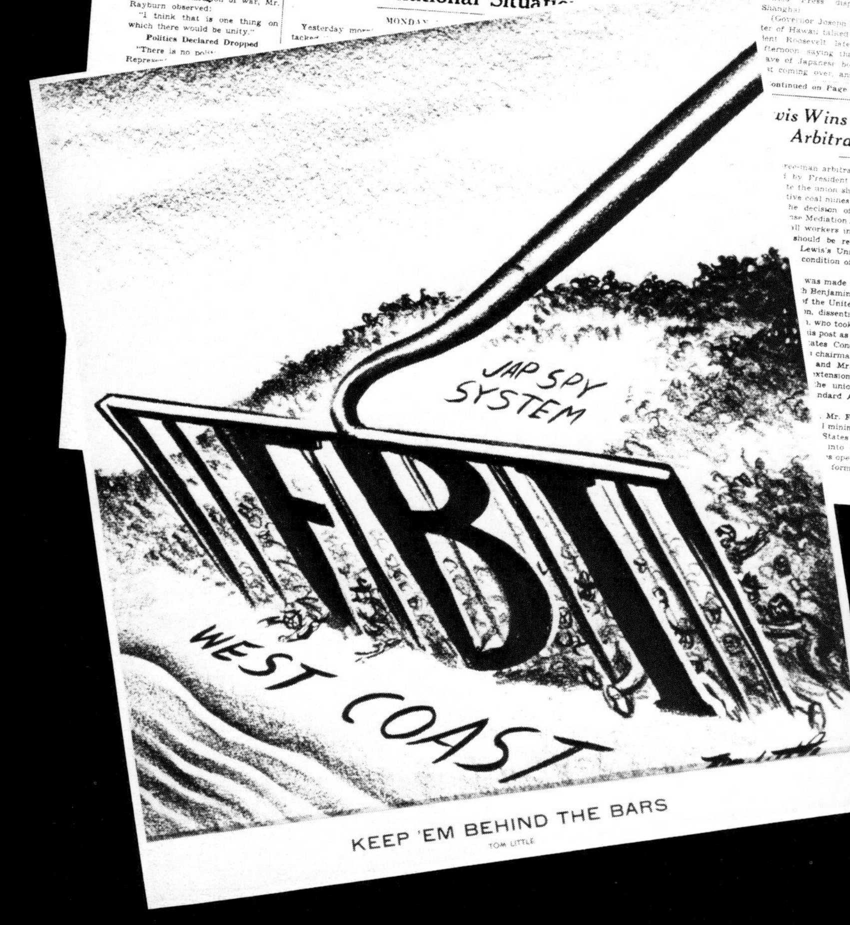

JAP SPY SYSTEM
FBI
WEST COAST
KEEP 'EM BEHIND THE BARS
TOM LITTLE

LEFT: An editorial cartoon applauding the FBI's round-up of Japanese aliens during World War II.

RIGHT: FBI agents escort Japanese, Italian and German aliens to Ellis Island at the opening of World War II.

BELOW: Japanese-Americans are marched under Army escort at a Seattle dock on their way to internment in California.

Before the United States even entered the war the FBI had been checking security at selected factories and had helped present education programs about sabotage. Within two years of declaration of war, the bureau had cranked its staff up from 2602 agents to 5072. The entire staff of the bureau went from about 7500 to more than 13,000, numbers that would be scaled back after the war ended.

Seventy-two hours after the start of the war, FBI agents and local police had rounded up nearly 4000 Japanese, German and Italian aliens considered most likely to be dangerous to wartime security of the nation. These were people the FBI had investigated individually. Unlike in World War I, those aliens had fairly quick access to legal counsel and were given the right to a hearing.

All that, however, did not stop one of the most appalling wartime rights abuses ever committed in this nation. Hoover objected, but the decision was made higher up to round up more than 100,000 people of Japanese heritage, most of them citizens of the United States, and to freeze their assets.

Hoover assessed the situation correctly when he said, 'The necessity for mass evacuation is based primarily upon public and political pressure rather than on factual data. Public hysteria and, in some instances, the comments of the press and radio announcers, have resulted in a tremendous amount of pressure. . . .'

In 1942 came the saboteur case that Hoover always called one of the best moments in the FBI's history. FBI agents arrested eight Germans who landed by submarine on Long Island and Florida with the intent of blowing up factories, railroads and the locks on major waterways. The would-be saboteurs carried a large amount of explosives and about $175,000 for their work. The case was broken with information provided by one of the Germans, not through tough FBI investigation. It was a fact that Hoover would barely acknowledge, as was so often true when a citizen or an informant helped solve a case.

In June 1942 the Germans, led by George Dasch, landed. Dasch had been in America for about 20 years, but he never became a citizen. He returned to Germany in 1941

BELOW: The huge Owens Valley Alien Reception Center in Manzanar, California, where Japanese residents of the United States were detained during the war.

when the Third Reich paid his way back. When Dasch and three other Germans landed on Long Island one night, they were spotted by a Coast Guard seaman. They got away from him, but the seaman reported what he had seen to the FBI.

But before the FBI could get anywhere with an investigation, Dasch and one of his companions, Ernest Burger, decided they wanted out of the game. Dasch called the New York FBI office, and then showed up at headquarters in Washington. He showed agents the money he brought and told them the whole tale. Within two weeks, FBI agents using Dasch's information had rounded up all eight of the Germans before they had committed even one act of sabotage. The arrests were extremely important because they persuaded German leaders to abandon the follow-up missions they already had planned.

Documents released to the public more than 40 years later showed that Dasch and his buddies didn't get the treatment Dasch expected. Dasch apparently was led to believe that all would get lenient treatment. Instead, they were convicted in secret trials of spying. Dasch got 30 years in prison, Burger got life, and the other six were led one by one to the District of Columbia's red oak electric chair without even being told of their sentence.

OPPOSITE TOP: Ernest Dasch, one of the eight Nazi saboteurs on trial in Washington, DC in 1942.

OPPOSITE BOTTOM: An FBI agent testifies during the Nazi saboteurs' trial.

RIGHT: A 1942 editorial cartoon showing the FBI upsetting Nazi sabotage plans.

Following the war, Dasch and Burger were released to Germany, where Dasch lived a hard life after Burger reported that Dasch had betrayed the Fatherland. When Dasch applied to return to the United States for a visit in the early 1980s, the State Department refused on the grounds that he had been convicted of enemy war crimes.

In 1946, President Harry S Truman presented J Edgar Hoover with the Medal of Merit for the FBI's work in foiling the sabotage mission. Hoover proudly wore the lapel pin representing that medal for many years afterward.

No matter what controversies emerged later, the difference between the bureau's work in the two world wars was obvious. No slacker raids, minimal vigilante action and very little, if any, sabotage occurred during World War II. That difference even earned a mention from the American Civil Liberties Union.

Tougher years were ahead. Keeping up with Soviet spies who infiltrated the United States would not be as easy. FBI agents would perform some heroic services, but also would be roundly criticized for civil rights abuses. The ACLU would not always praise them.

The end of the war also signaled an end to some of the Federal Bureau of Investigation's official duties. Sabotage was not so much a worry now, and, much to Hoover's chagrin, his bureau was relieved of its Western hemisphere espionage duties outside the United States. President Harry S Truman established the National Intelligence Authority, the forerunner of the Central Intelligence Agency, to take over that job. That was the end of the FBI's Special Intelligence Authority, which had done anti-Nazi work in Central and South America during the war.

The bureau hardly was inactive, however. Among what some would consider the more trivial work was checking on claims and fraud against the government. A favorite story, oft repeated, was the World War II veteran who claimed he was totally and permanently disabled as a result of the war. He wanted his insurance payments. He never got them. A bureau agent spent several days quietly observing the man on his farm. He watched the fellow plow, pick up heavy sacks and run down some mules that got away from him. He took pictures of all of the above back with him.

More desperate were the fights against an increasing crime rate and against a rise in communism and communist spying. The rising crime rate was hard to peg. Some crime certainly was tied to the migration from the farm to the cities that started about the time of the war and has continued since. Hoover also linked some of it to a fundamental change in home life that happened when father went to war and mother worked in the factories. Children were left to their own devices.

Hoover had addressed juvenile delinquency before, but suddenly he had a new forum for his views. '. . . If a child can be reached by the adults around him and fortified with the fundamental values of good citizenship, he will come through successfully in spite of adverse conditions that may surround him,' he wrote in *The Rotarian* in 1945. In the *Syracuse Law Review* he said, 'Criminal behavior is learned behavior. The child and the adolescent are impressionable, and their active minds develop codes of morality no higher than those to which they are exposed. The environment which the adult community provides its growing children is the most important factor underlying the behavior patterns cultivated by the normal child.' The importance of the nuclear family in the prevention of juvenile delinquency would remain an important topic for Hoover for the rest of his life.

The crime increase could be seen in the

ABOVE: The Boys Anti-Crime Council of New York City visiting FBI headquarters. Hoover addressed juvenile delinquency as an aspect of the rising crime rate.

OPPOSITE: Hoover with long-time aide Clyde Tolson in 1947.

statistics. Population rose 24 percent between 1945 and 1955, but crime increased nearly 45 percent. Major crimes – those involving murder, rape, manslaughter, robbery, aggravated assault, burglary, larceny and automobile theft – rose above the two million mark for the first time in 1952. Included in those figures was an enormous rise in juvenile crime.

Just as important to Hoover was the domestic battle against communists. Hoover had formed his fears of and opinions about communism during 1919, and those views had changed little. Communist Party membership in the United States had grown to what then was an all-time high during the war. And before anyone in the country even knew what was happening, Soviet spies had stolen vital atomic energy information. The situation did call for drastic action at the time, but in the 1950s the red hunt would ruin many an innocent man as hysteria spread across the nation.

During this postwar period the FBI acquired more and more responsibility for checking on the loyalty and background of federal employees. It was legitimate work, but it also occasionally brought about legitimate questions. Included in the bureau's raw files, files that were not supposed to see the light of day unless certain information was proven, were numerous names provided on hearsay or for purposes of pure revenge. Unfortunately, information in those

files sometimes slipped out. It is one of the major controversies about the bureau that continues today.

The most notable victory for the FBI in the 1940s came at the end of the decade when 11 top leaders of the Communist Party of the United States of America were convicted of conspiracy to overthrow the government. When the trial opened on 17 January 1949, the leaders suddenly realized that the FBI had been spying on them for at least 10 years, and that one of their most trusted compatriots, Herbert A Philbrick, had been working undercover for the bureau since the early 1940s. Not even Philbrick's wife knew of the double life. In all, six undercover informants testified. The communist movement would remain riddled with informants for years to come.

The international communist conspiracy is 'clearly the greatest menace free civilization has known . . .,' Hoover told Congress in the 1950s. 'The seriousness of the

BELOW: In July 1948, FBI agents arrested six top leaders of the Communist Party in the United States and charged them with conspiring to overthrow the government.

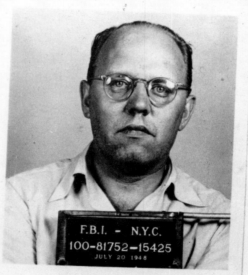

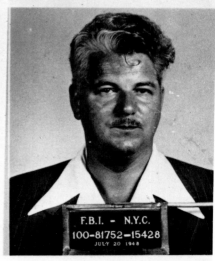

domestic threat from a Soviet-dominated communist party in the United States bears a relationship proportionate to the world threat posed by its masters in the Soviet Union and must be gauged accordingly.'

As that trial closed down, Americans were going through or were about to go through two spy cases that would shake them deeply. The FBI had investigative responsibilities in both the spy cases. The reaction to those cases would contribute directly to yet another dark chapter in the nation's history – Joe McCarthy's vicious red hunts.

ABOVE: Herbert Philbrick, who worked nine years as an FBI undercover agent inside the Communist Party, testifies before a Senate subcommittee in 1953.

CHAPTER FIVE

LIBERTY AND JUSTICE FOR ALL: THE 1950S

You hear about constitutional rights, free speech and the free press. Every time I hear those words I say to myself, 'That man is a red!' You never hear a real American talk like that.

Although former mayor of Jersey City, New Jersey, Frank Hague's sentiments were expressed during the 1940s, they were words that well-expressed the mood that swept the American political landscape in the decade that followed. Communism at home and abroad generated a wind of fear and hatred that resulted in a whirlwind of demagogy and political exploitation. The struggle between justice and liberty in America never raged hotter than during the 1950s.

Communist forces were trying to overrun Korea and the public was stunned by revelations from the spy trials of Julius and Ethel Rosenberg, Harry Gold and Klaus Fuchs. Suddenly, Russia also had the atomic bomb. Senator Joseph McCarthy, Republican of Minnesota, warned of reds running rampant in the federal government. The times were ripe for full-bore commie-bashing, an activity at which no one could easily upstage J Edgar Hoover.

Hoover may have had a different perspective on constitutional rights than Frank Hague and his tactics may have differed

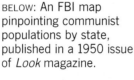

BELOW: An FBI map pinpointing communist populations by state, published in a 1950 issue of *Look* magazine.

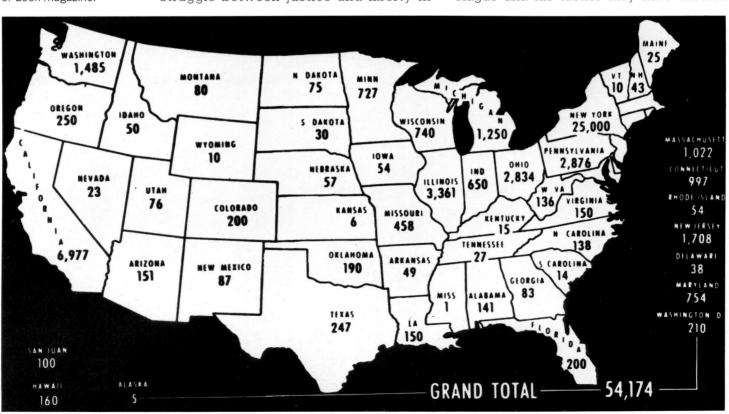

from those of Senator McCarthy, but the battle against communists was to become his and the FBI's. More than any other issue, the fight against the hordes of reds would come to define the FBI during a good part of the 1950s. Hoover never backed down from the cause, even when he came under pressure for oppressive surveillance and investigatory tactics used against innocent citizens. He had the support of most Americans, even those who watched McCarthy ruin innocent lives.

The battle against communism was a life-long crusade for Hoover. It started in 1919 when Hoover, as head of the Justice Department's General Intelligence Division, conducted the first government study of communism and its goals. His conclusion that Moscow was the center of a conspiracy to overthrow all world governments remained with him for the rest of his life.

Because one of the FBI's duties was to stop subversion in the United States, Hoover's penchant for hunting down domestic

BELOW: Hoover testified before the Senate Internal Security Subcommittee in 1953.

ABOVE: A communist
official briefs the press at
the party's national
convention in New York in
1957.

communists had the sanction of law. Given the national mood, the director's ideological bent and the power of the FBI, it was inevitable that the agency would play a major role in the red-baiting that dominated the decade.

Communism seemed to be on everyone's mind. In Birmingham, Alabama, local officials outlawed from the city anyone discovered talking to a communist in a non-public place. Other cities outlawed the sale of subversive literature. Marauding 'patriots' beat up suspected communists and threw rocks at the homes of those known to be officials in legal communist groups. Vigilante action got so bad that President Harry S Truman had to remind people that suspected subversion should be reported to authorities who would then investigate and decide what action, if any, to take.

Some of the paranoia apparently was justified. In the 1930s and early 1940s the American Communist Party boasted a membership of 80,000 or better. The figure, according to FBI estimates, had dropped to 43,000 by 1950, 20,000 by 1955 and less than 10,000 by the early 1960s. Some of the decrease can be attributed to disillusionment caused when American communists realized what was happening during Joseph

Stalin's purges in Russia. The increased radicalism of the American Communist Party also contributed to the drop in interest among the more moderate hangers-on.

The FBI also got its share of the credit for depleting the ranks of American communists, however. Robert F Kennedy, when he was attorney general in the early 1960s and was barely speaking to Hoover, said, 'A major reason for the numerical weakness and lack of broad influence of the Communist Party in the United States is the dedication and effort of J Edgar Hoover and the FBI. Those who dismiss the problem of Soviet espionage perform a disservice to the nation.'

By the time Kennedy praised the FBI, though, the Communist Party was hardly a threat. The bureau had so riddled it with informants that party officials once appointed an FBI spy to weed out informants from the party. He had a field day clearing the real informants while framing those loyal to the communists.

Two cases in the late 1940s and the early 1950s fired up the American public and helped push red scare paranoia beyond the limits. Both cases involved either government employees or government programs.

The FBI's involvement with government loyalty checks started meekly in 1939 with the Hatch Act, which made it illegal for any government employee to belong to a party or organization advocating the overthrow of the government. The FBI, however, could not undertake an investigation of an individual unless so requested by the head of the agency where the person worked.

In 1947, President Truman established the Federal Employees Loyalty Program and a Loyalty Review Board. Under the program, the FBI checked the name of every executive branch employee against its records for any hints of potential disloyalty. Full investigation came only when the FBI found negative information in its files or when a specific allegation was received. During the loyalty program's five-year life, the FBI checked on three million people and ran 10,000 full field investigations.

The loyalty program brought the government and the FBI under assault for violation of civil rights. The murmurs grew to a near roar after the espionage case against government employee Judith Coplon opened some FBI raw investigative files and showed the world how the agency collected gossip and unsubstantiated charges during the course of an inquiry. The opening of the Coplon files brought to light the names of people who were mentioned during the in-

ABOVE: An editorial cartoon of 1953 showing the Hoover Dam holding back the Red Tide.

LEFT: A registration form for communists required by the Communist Control Act, signed by President Dwight D Eisenhower in 1954.

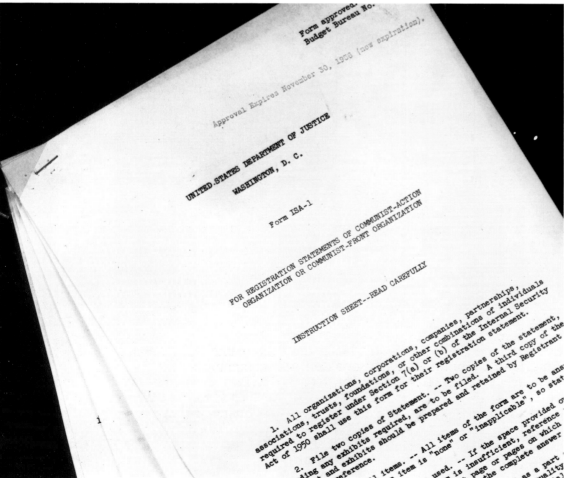

vestigation but who were innocent of any wrongdoing.

The FBI had tried to prevent the release of the files, but US Attorney General Tom C Clark ordered their use in Coplon's trial. Coplon was convicted of espionage with a Soviet agent, but the decision was overturned due to the fact that she was nabbed by the FBI without the benefit of an arrest warrant.

Some of the criticism of the agency and the loyalty program was forgotten when the Whittaker Chambers-Alger Hiss case broke into the headlines. The details truly shocked the nation and sent out ripples of controversy that would continue for years.

In 1948, Whittaker Chambers, a former *Time* magazine editor and freelance writer, went before the House Committee on Un-American Activities and told members that not only had he been a member of the Communist Party for 13 years, he also had dealt stolen government documents to the Soviets. One of his accomplices, he said, was Alger Hiss, who had been a rising star in the State Department. Hiss was president

of the Carnegie Institute for World Peace when he was accused.

His career was astounding. He was a Phi Beta Kappa graduate of Johns Hopkins University, a Harvard Law School graduate, and had been secretary to Oliver Wendell Holmes and law clerk for Felix Frankfurter. He did important work in the founding of the United Nations and was an aide to the secretary of state at the Yalta conference.

Hiss denied all the allegations and even sued Chambers for libel after Chambers repeated his charges on *Meet the Press*. Hiss has maintained his innocence ever since, even after being convicted of perjury for saying he did not know Chambers and that he did not pass secrets to the Russians.

The FBI was the investigative agency on the claims and counterclaims. More than 230 agents worked on the case at one time or another. Agents tracked down a typewriter they said belonged to Hiss in the 1930s. Some of Chambers' incriminating documents had been typed on the machine. Using only a portrait and a name, they tracked down a former maid for the Chambers' who said she remembered seeing Hiss and Chambers together. Agents put together other circumstantial evidence that Hiss knew Chambers and that he passed information to him.

The typewriter was particularly important, and Hiss has always denied it belonged to him. He also charged that the FBI knew it

TOP RIGHT: A 1950s editorial cartoon of Hoover locking out subversive 'rats.'

RIGHT: Whittaker Chambers, a protagonist in the Hiss/Chambers trial, leaving the Federal Court Building in New York.

OPPOSITE TOP: A 1947 editorial cartoon on the Federal Employees Loyalty Program.

OPPOSITE BOTTOM: In this 1948 press conference at his New York City apartment, Alger Hiss admitted he knew Whittaker Chambers but said he had no link with the Communist Party.

ABOVE: Alger Hiss, standing at the right, confronts Whittaker Chambers, standing far left, during a 1948 hearing of the House Committee on Un-American Activities.

RIGHT: Julius Rosenberg and his wife, Ethel, leaving federal court in a marshal's van after their conviction on espionage charges in March 1951. They were executed in 1953.

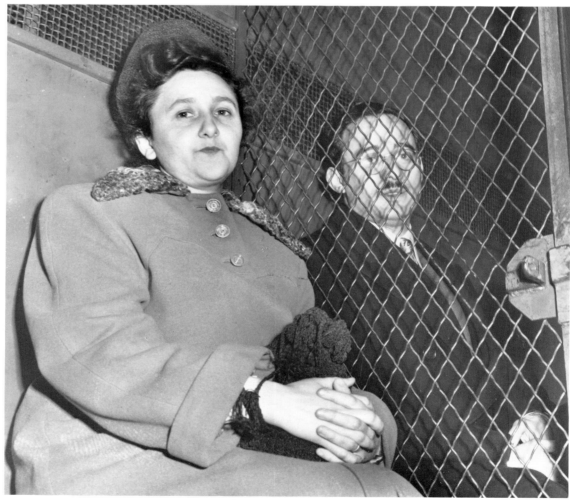

could not have belonged to him, that FBI agents coached the maid on her testimony, and knew that she lied on the witness stand. Hiss' first trial, in 1949, ended in a hung jury. In 1950, he was convicted and was sentenced to five years in prison. He was released in 1954.

By the time of the Hiss trials, the Cold War and red fear was running strong. The hysteria heightened even more when it was discovered that American atomic secrets had been passed to the Soviets years earlier, and that the United States no longer had a monopoly on the bomb. Although the Russians are likely to have eventually developed their own atomic bomb without the stolen information, few Americans at the time were willing to believe Russia had the scientific talent to create the weapon unassisted. The general public believed that the people accused of passing the secrets had sold America to its doom.

The revelations about the atomic spy ring eventually led to the execution of husband and wife Julius and Ethel Rosenberg in 1953 for helping mastermind the passing of information. Both pled their innocence to the end. It appears, in fact, that government prosecutors never meant for Ethel Rosenberg to die, and actually had a weak case against her. They were trying to use her death sentence to get a confession out of Julius Rosenberg in return for sparing her life. He refused, saying there was nothing to confess.

Hoover called it 'the crime of the century.' Judge Irving Kaufman, who sentenced the Rosenbergs, called their activities 'worse than murder,' and he accused them of causing the Korean War. The sentence, however, was obviously a reaction to the Cold War times. Future spies such as the Walker family, who did as much or more damage, were not executed. And it was another spy by the name of Dr Klaus Fuchs who actually did the most damage to America's atomic secrets.

The trial and its revelations were stunning by any measure. Fuchs' arrest in Great Britain came first. He had been a member of the British scientific team working in America on the bomb during World War II, first in New York and then at Los Alamos, New Mexico. The FBI interviewed Fuchs in England and came back with information that he had passed secrets to a man named Harry Gold, who was a chemist, in 1945. Gold then took the secrets to a Soviet contact. Fuchs eventually was sentenced to 14 years in prison in Great Britain, which does not have a death penalty.

The FBI went to work. Three days after

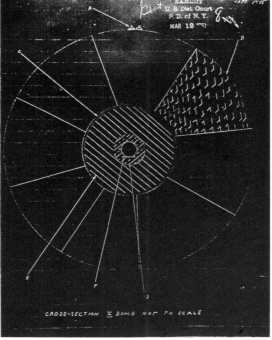

ABOVE: Federal agents escort Julius Rosenberg to an interrogation session in July 1950.

LEFT: The atomic bomb sketch the Rosenbergs allegedly delivered to the Soviets in 1945.

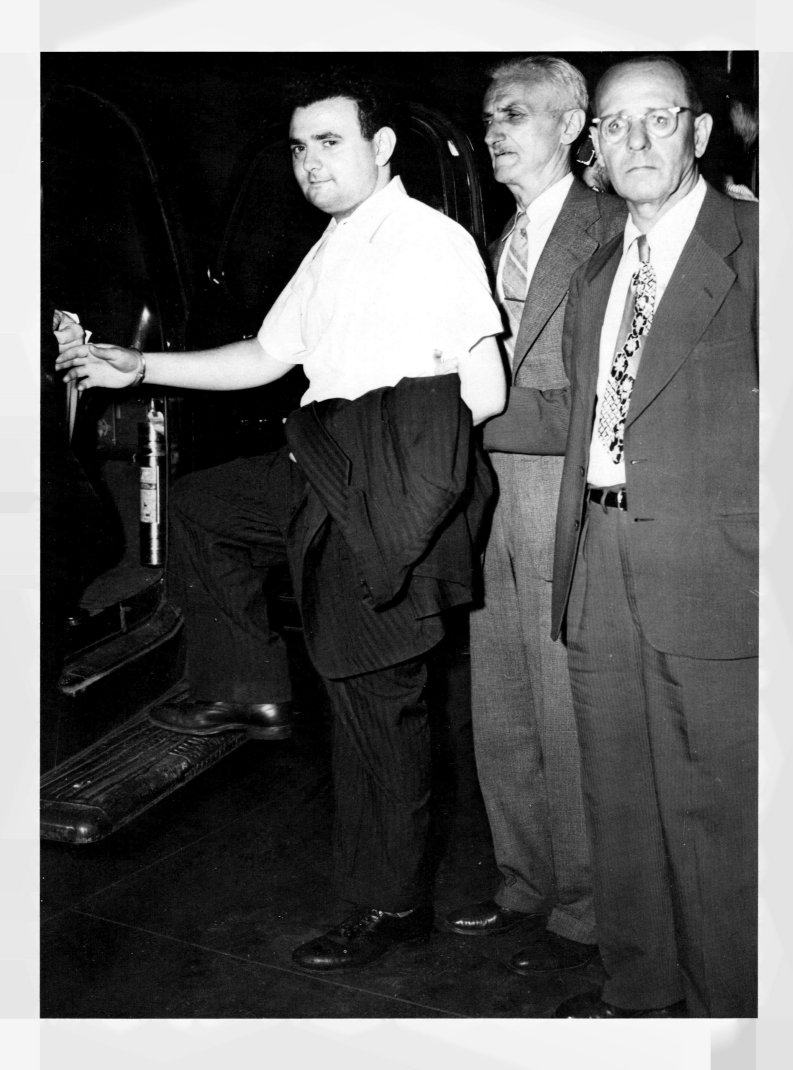

RIGHT: Rosenberg sympathizers demonstrate in hopes of saving the couple from execution.

OPPOSITE: Also charged with atomic espionage in connection with the Rosenberg case was David Greenglass, shown here being escorted back to a New York jail after an appearance before a grand jury.

BOTTOM LEFT: A confession by Dr Klaus Fuchs led to the breaking of the Rosenberg case.

BOTTOM RIGHT: Hoover offers his opinions on atomic security to the Joint Atomic Energy Committee in June 1950.

ABOVE: Michael and Robert Meeropol, sons of Ethel and Julius Rosenberg, demonstrated outside the New York Supreme Court in 1975, demanding a reopening of the trial transcripts to prove their parents were 'railroaded.'

an implosion bomb and gave vague details about how it worked.

The FBI worked hard at tracking down physical evidence, but much that was presented at the trial consisted of replicas of key documents. They found items such as a hotel registration card, bank records and a Communist Party nominating petition signed by Ethel Rosenberg in 1939. Rosenberg supporters, of which there were few in the early 1950s, argued that Ruth and David Greenglass were sacrificing Julius and Ethel Rosenberg to save themselves. The jurors thought the evidence damning, and they voted for conviction.

The FBI continued up until the execution to try to get a confession from Julius Rosenberg in return for sparing Ethel Rosenberg's life. They never got it, and on 19 June 1953 the couple went to the electric chair shortly after 8 PM. They left behind two young sons, who to this day continue a battle to clear the names of their parents. David Greenglass went to prison for 15 years, and Harry Gold was sentenced to 30 years.

On 9 February 1950, J Edgar Hoover was joined in his hunt for communists by Senator Joseph McCarthy of Wisconsin. Hoover was delighted at first, and, although he denied it, he willingly fed McCarthy information through intermediaries. Later, when McCarthy's witch hunts were being discredited, Hoover discreetly distanced himself from the man.

Hoover and the FBI did score some successes fighting communism in the United States; McCarthy, for the most part, merely destroyed the lives and careers of innocent people. McCarthy may truly have despised communism, but his campaign was simply the most public of many designed to hitch on to the anticommunism bandwagon.

McCarthy's famous opening salvo took place in Wheeling, West Virginia, in a speech to Republicans there.

'While I cannot take the time to name all the men in the State Department who have been named as active members of the Communist Party and members of a spy ring, I have here in my hand a list of 205 – a list of names that were made known to the secretary of state as being members of the Communist Party and who nevertheless are still working and shaping policy in the State Department.'

He would not show anybody the list that night; he in fact had no list in his hand. But the announcement hit with the impact of an atomic bomb on a public that was willing to believe anything, given the red hysteria of the time.

agents returned from England on 23 May 1950, they arrested Gold. The trail went on and several arrests followed, including that of David and Ruth Greenglass, Ethel Rosenberg's brother and sister-in-law. Julius Rosenberg was arrested the day after David Greenglass, and Ethel Rosenberg was arrested two months later.

Most of the FBI's strongest evidence came from the Greenglasses, who testified that Julius Rosenberg recruited David to supply information while David was working as a machinist at Los Alamos. He said that he gave Julius Rosenberg and Gold a rough sketch of a high explosive lens mold, one of the key parts to making the bomb work. He also drew from memory a sketch of

It appears now that much of McCarthy's information during his red hunts came from FBI reports gathered during their infiltration of communist groups or suspected communist groups, and during their questioning of spies or suspected spies. Most of those were names of people suspected of unpatriotic tendencies or actions, suspicions which had not been, or could not be, proven.

McCarthy eventually lost Hoover's support when he told senate questioners that he based his accusations on charts prepared by the FBI. Regardless of whether the claim was true, it was a breach of rules and protocol for the FBI to have provided any such chart, and Hoover denied it. Hoover apparently did provide information to McCarthy, but he did it by passing documents to military intelligence, which then passed it on to the senator.

McCarthy's tactics usually took the form of smearing people who years before had belonged to an organization, such as the American Civil Liberties Union, that some believed was a communist front. It did not matter whether or not the target knew of the suspicion or whether or not the accused had ever done anything illegal. It also did not matter whether or not the group actually was a communist front; it only mattered that someone, somewhere made the accusation. He also cast suspicion on people who either disagreed with his views or who invoked the Fifth Amendment under questioning.

McCarthy's fall started when he hooked into the Rosenberg case by claiming that a spy ring set up by Rosenberg at the United States Signal Corps laboratories at Fort Monmouth, New Jersey, might still be in operation. The claim came 10 years after Rosenberg worked there as a civilian and four months after his execution at Sing Sing.

As with most of McCarthy's investigations, this one created a major storm but turned up no evidence of a spy ring or spies. Nonetheless, more than 30 Fort Monmouth

BELOW: Army counsel Joseph N Welch, left, challenged Senator Joseph McCarthy as 'a cruelly reckless character assassin' during the Army-McCarthy hearings at the height of McCarthy's red scare.

RIGHT: McCarthy's credibility fell apart during the highly-publicized Army hearings.

employees were suspended and it was several years before they were able to win their jobs back. The information on the so-called spy ring at Fort Monmouth apparently came to McCarthy from the FBI.

The Monmouth debacle led quickly to the Army-McCarthy hearings, where the senator's credibility was destroyed. He was censured by the Senate in 1954, started drinking heavily and died in 1957. While most decry McCarthy's tactics, some today still consider him a hero who was needed during a dangerous time.

J Edgar Hoover's years of investigating, studying and writing about communists culminated in 1958 with his book, *Masters of Deceit*. Considered high camp by some today, the book gravely explained the communists' plans for the United States and told how they were going about trying to take over the nation. The book also gave a summary of communist history and thumbnail sketches of important men such as Karl Marx, Vladimir I Lenin and Joseph Stalin.

One chapter of the book explains how communists keep their affiliations hidden. It explains elaborate steps taken to establish hideouts and safe meeting places and tells the reader how reds go about determining whether they are being followed by car or on foot. A viewer of any spy movie has seen it all on the screen; entering crowded buildings with many exits, leaving subways at the last second as the doors are closing, or waiting until oncoming traffic is close before making a left turn in front of it.

Hoover warned the nation that the stereotype of the bumbling Soviet spy no longer fit. He discussed several ways one

BELOW: McCarthy was censured by the Senate in 1954, began drinking heavily and died in 1957.

ABOVE: Hoover testifying before the House Un-American Activities Committee in March 1947.

OPPOSITE: Federal authorities investigate the 1955 bombing of a United Airlines plane near Denver that killed 44 people.

might spot communists or determine whether an organization was a communist front. In what could be considered a disclaimer tuned toward the excesses of the McCarthy era, Hoover's 1958 book cautions that, while the FBI wants to hear about suspicious activities, it does not want people to be reported on the basis of holding an unpopular or minority opinion.

Using his high public profile, Hoover also attacked other situations that bothered him

during the 1950s. He railed against light sentences and early parole for criminals, and his concern about juvenile delinquency came up time and time again. 'The present youth problem does not involve child pranksters and mischief-makers. We can no longer afford to let "tender age" make plunder into a trifling prank, reduce mayhem to a mischievous act, and pass off murder as a boyish misdemeanor or the act of an emotionally disturbed youth,' he told the House

ABOVE: FBI agents guard John Gilbert Graham, 23, charged with bombing the United Airlines plane and killing 44 people. Graham was convicted and later executed.

OPPOSITE TOP: Graham's mother, Mrs Daisy King, was among the 44 killed in the crash.

OPPOSITE BOTTOM: Graham sits impassively in the witness box during his sentencing.

Appropriations Committee in 1959.

The FBI was instrumental in breaking some important cases in the 1950s. When United Airlines Passenger Flight 629 exploded, killing 44 people, after leaving Denver's Stapleton Airport on 1 November 1955, FBI agents cracked the case within two weeks. It was a classic example of scientific investigation and shrewd questioning. Agents started by identifying the mutilated victims through fingerprints. Meanwhile, other evidence technicians collected pieces of the plane and any luggage that could be found. Reconstruction of the plane showed that a hole had been blown in the fuselage in the cargo pit. A check of air freight shipments for the flight showed no explosives, and the FBI laboratory found residues that clearly indicated a dynamite explosion had wreaked the havoc.

While lab technicians worked, other agents started checking the backgrounds of the people who were killed, particularly taking into account the more than $750,000 in insurance policies for those on board.

One woman who was killed, Daisie King, was carrying clippings that showed that her son, Jack Graham, had been convicted of forgery in 1951 and for a while had been on the FBI's Most Wanted list. Very little of Mrs King's luggage was found, flagging it as a possible source of the explosion.

It was soon discovered that Graham stood to inherit a sizeable estate and a good amount of insurance money that had hurriedly been taken out just before the flight. Further background checks showed that Jack Graham had often been a troublesome son. A drive-in his mother owned had been wrecked by an explosion, for which insurance money had been paid, and his pickup truck had once 'stalled' in front of a train. Insurance money was paid again.

Evidence continued to build. Interviews with people at the airport showed that Graham seemed especially nervous while seeing his mother off, and that he had fumbled and made mistakes when taking out the insurance policies on his mother's life. After the plane took off, he suddenly got sick. When he and his wife learned of the crash as they were leaving the airport coffee shop he said, 'That's it. Let's go home.' Clearly, the FBI had cause to question Graham.

Agents quickly caught him in lies. He told them he did not put anything in his mother's luggage because she was fussy about the way her suitcases should be packed. His wife said, however, that he had been looking for a set of tools for his mother's hobby of making costume jewelry from sea shells, and that he had a gift-wrapped package that she assumed was the tool set. She also assumed he had put it in her luggage. A check of the Denver area stores that sold that type of tools showed that no one had purchased such a kit during October.

With Graham's permission they searched his home and found insulated copper wire like that used to detonate primer caps. They also found the shotgun shells and rifle ammunition Graham had earlier said was in his mother's luggage. He had implied that the ammunition may have caused the explosion. Faced with overwhelming evidence, Graham finally confessed on 14 November. He had made a time bomb using 25 sticks of dynamite wired to a timer and a six-volt battery.

Even with a signed confession the agents continued to pile up evidence. They wanted to make sure that if Graham repudiated his confession, which he eventually did, they would have enough evidence to convict him anyway. They found the merchants who

sold Graham the timing device, the blasting caps and the dynamite and they even found a credit manager who said Graham had commented offhand about how easy it would be to blow up an airplane. Also as expected, Graham claimed he was insane. Two court-appointed psychiatrists and two others hired by the defense disagreed. A jury took only 69 minutes to convict Graham and sentence him to death. He went to the gas chamber on 11 January 1957.

In 1956 the Peter Weinberger kidnaping case would fundamentally change the rules under which the FBI could enter kidnaping investigations. One-month-old Peter Weinberger was kidnaped from his family's patio in Westbury, Long Island, when his mother left him alone there for a few moments in July 1956. The kidnaper left a note apologizing and telling the parents to leave $2000 at a certain signpost the next day.

The FBI was not allowed on the case immediately because federal law required a seven-day waiting period before agents could presume the kidnap victim had been taken across state lines. And kidnaping, as is true with some other crimes, is not a federal matter until a state line has been crossed.

Local police took control of the case. The story was soon leaked to the New York

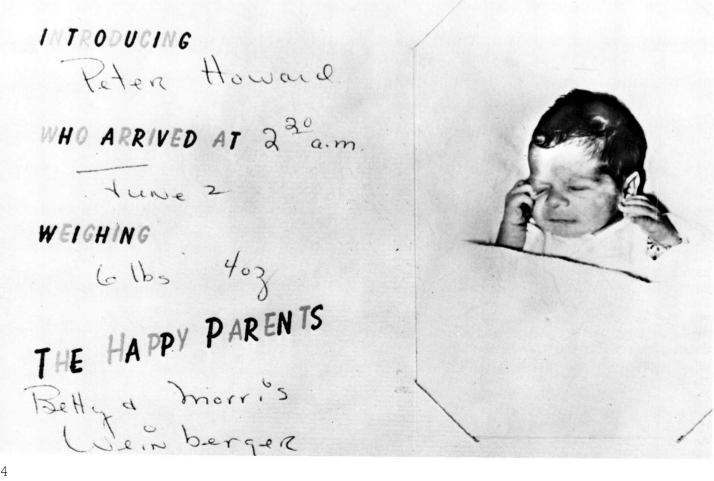

OPPOSITE TOP: The kidnapers of one-month-old Peter Weinberger failed to pick up the ransom money in the envelope beneath this tree in Long Island in 1956.

OPPOSITE BOTTOM: Peter Weinberger's birth announcement.

ABOVE: Investigators point to the spot where the Weinberger baby's body was found in August 1956.

RIGHT: The note from the Weinberger kidnap case.

newspapers, and reporters immediately began hounding police for leads. Police asked the journalists to hold the story until after the ransom deadline the next day, in the hope that the kidnaper would collect the ransom and return the child. All but one newspaper, the *Daily News*, agreed to the embargo. The *News* beat its competition to the street with a brief bulletin in its early edition, followed by a full-blown front page treatment with banner headline and juicy details. The break of the story released the other newspapers from their pledge, and in no time a full account of the crime was everywhere.

The next morning the crime scene and the ransom pickup point were swarming with journalists and sightseers. Nassau County Chief of Detectives Stuyvesant Pin-

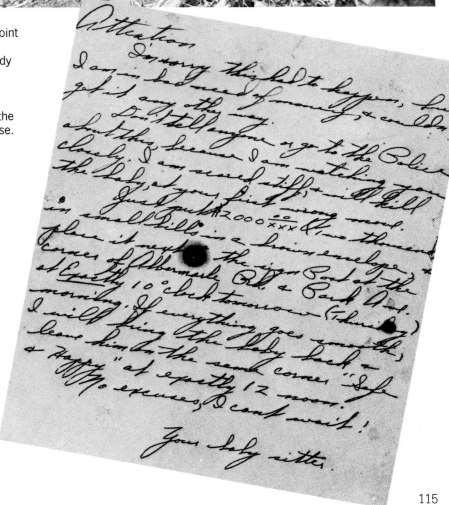

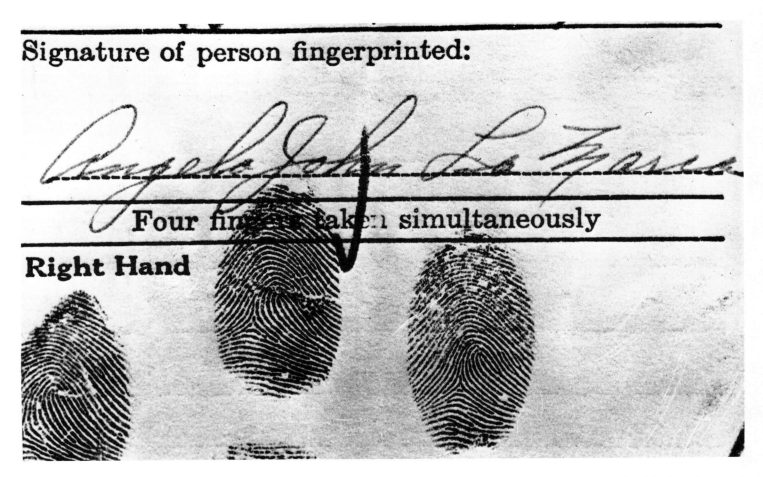

Signature of person fingerprinted:

Four fingers taken simultaneously

Right Hand

ABOVE: The signature and fingerprints of Angelo John La Marca, a Long Island cab driver accused of kidnaping Peter Weinberger.

OPPOSITE: FBI agents bring La Marca to police headquarters in Mineola, New York, after his capture in August 1956.

nell later said, 'We would have got a hell of a lot further if there had been no interference from the press.' Pinnell's opinion turned out to be an understatement. Weeks later it was learned that the kidnaper brought the baby, alive and well, to the ransom pickup point, but had fled when he saw all the commotion. He dropped the baby in a thicket near Plainview, where little Peter died.

FBI investigators, after waiting the required seven days, got to enter the case long after every curious sightseer in New York had already explored the crime scene. Agents had only one clue, but it was enough. The handwriting of the kidnaper was distinctive, and agents started looking for something similar. They eventually screened two million documents, checking, among others, auto registrations, voting records and loan company documents. On his second visit to the United States Probation Office in Brooklyn, an agent found the handwriting he was looking for, that of Angelo John LaMarca, a Plainview man who had once been convicted of bootlegging.

When confronted with the handwriting evidence the next day, LaMarca broke down and confessed, telling agents of his desperate need for cash. And he told them the heartbreaking story of dropping the baby in the weeds after seeing the swarm of people near the ransom pickup point.

LaMarca was convicted of kidnaping and murder in 1956, and died in the electric chair at Sing Sing Prison in 1958.

As a direct result of the mishandling of the Weinberger case, Congress amended the Federal Kidnaping Act to allow the FBI to enter a case after 24 hours. Even that law change would not have done any good in the Weinberger case, because LaMarca had been frightened away less than 24 hours after he snatched little Peter. But with the change, the FBI was now allowed to move more quickly. Just four months later, the FBI had already intervened in 17 kidnapings that were resolved in one way or another before the old seven-day presumptive clause would have allowed them to act.

By the late 1950s, the FBI was already involved in other areas that would take up a lot of their time during the 1960s and would cause plenty of controversy. The push was on to get the agency to help protect the rights of blacks and to investigate the Mafia. For a time, Hoover refused to acknowledge that the Mafia existed, and he insisted that his agents had no right to interfere with the role of the states in civil rights matters. He was wrong about the Mafia, but it would take some federal law changes to help his agents in the battle against the Cosa Nostra. And his agency would eventually take a partial role in the civil rights fight.

CHAPTER SIX

THE TURBULENT 1960S

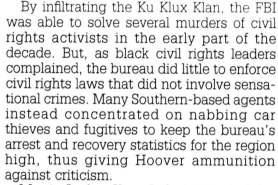

The turbulent storm of the 1960s that shook America with the news of the brutal, often lethal, clash of Freedom Riders with Southern segregationists and numbed the nation with the anguish of a presidential assassination, also rattled the foundation of the Federal Bureau of Investigation. The FBI, under an aging J Edgar Hoover, struggled with limited success to keep pace with the fast-moving 1960s. On the civil rights front, Hoover's agency spent most of its time and energy walking the narrow line between those crying for government protection from racial violence on one side, and, on the other, staunch states' rights advocates bristling at federal interference with Southern tradition.

By infiltrating the Ku Klux Klan, the FBI was able to solve several murders of civil rights activists in the early part of the decade. But, as black civil rights leaders complained, the bureau did little to enforce civil rights laws that did not involve sensational crimes. Many Southern-based agents instead concentrated on nabbing car thieves and fugitives to keep the bureau's arrest and recovery statistics for the region high, thus giving Hoover ammunition against criticism.

Martin Luther King Jr first attracted the attention of J Edgar Hoover in February 1961, when the young Baptist minister, quoted in an article in the *Nation,* made a passing reference to the FBI in calling for the elimination of racial discrimination in federal employment and urging greater representation of blacks in federal police agencies. Bureau officials decided it 'inadvisable' to challenge King's mild comments about the agency's hiring policies. Two months later, however, when the State Department notified the FBI that King was being considered for appointment to an advisory committee on African affairs, the bureau responded with a negative recommendation.

In May 1961, as King emerged as one of the organizers of the Freedom Riders demonstrating for desegregation in the South, Hoover called for information on King and the other leaders. When the director was informed by memorandum that 'King has not been investigated by the FBI,' he scrawled 'Why not?' in the memo margin and called for more details. Investigators soon reported that Stanley David Levison, a New York lawyer who had had ties with the American Communist Party in the 1950s, was a friend and close advisor of the Reverend King. The FBI had for a while kept

tabs on Levison, but had given him little attention since trying unsuccessfully to recruit him as an informant after he apparently dropped his communist associations in the late 1950s. His connection with the civil rights movement and King renewed the bureau's interest.

In January 1962 Hoover informed Attorney General Robert Kennedy (with whom he shared an intense mutual dislike and distrust) that Levison (whom he described as 'a member of the Communist Party USA' despite indications from bureau informants that Levison had discontinued his party involvement) was a close associate of King. Kennedy immediately dispatched one of his assistants to tell King, without mentioning names, that a close advisor of his was believed to have communist ties. (The bureau had expressed the fear that naming Levison might jeopardize an FBI informant.) King's response was that he was not aware of any such connection but that he did not question the motives of those who chose to support his cause.

In March 1962 Hoover, with the approval of Attorney General Kennedy, ordered a wiretap placed on Levison's office telephone. The director made regular reports of the intercepted conversations to the attorney general. The information yielded no evidence of communist infiltration or control of the Southern Christian Leadership Conference, and simply confirmed the fact that Levison was one of King's close advisors.

The communist background of another civil rights activist close to King, Jack O'Dell, intensified Hoover's interest in looking for evidence that the civil rights movement generally, and King specifically, might be influenced by the Communist Party. Levison, the bureau learned, had recommended O'Dell for a top executive spot in the SCLC, cautioning King about O'Dell's past communist ties. King said that was of no concern as long as the man could stand up and say he had renounced those past associations.

By November, the FBI got RFK's approval to put a tap on Levison's home phone. The conversations intercepted by the second tap were as innocuous as those from the first, but Robert Kennedy remained concerned about the effect that a communist connection might have on the outcome of the civil rights movement. He shared his concern with his brother in the Oval Office.

On 17 June 1963, after a meeting with the

civil rights leadership in the White House, President John Kennedy took the Reverend King for a stroll in the Rose Garden and bluntly told him that his continued association with Levison and O'Dell could scuttle the administration's civil rights legislative efforts, once their past communist connections became known. King reacted by formally removing O'Dell from his executive post in the SCLC office in New York (although O'Dell apparently continued his work with the office for a while after the decision was announced.) King also insulated his contact with Levison by simply going through a mutual friend, Clarence Jones, to talk with his advisor. King made no real move to sever ties with either O'Dell or Levison.

The FBI quickly caught on to the King-Jones-Levison communications network and put a tap on the phone at Jones' suburban New York home. By chance, King stayed at Jones' home for three days in August 1963. On 13 August, Hoover sent a two-page memorandum to the attorney general detailing information gleaned from the phone tap, mostly about King's personal life and sexual activities. A week later, Robert Kennedy passed the memo to his

ABOVE: President John F Kennedy convened a special White House conference on civil rights in June 1963. Pictured here in the Rose Garden are, left to right, Dr King, Robert Kennedy, Roy Wilkins (executive director of the NAACP), and Vice President Lyndon Johnson.

LEFT: Dr King waves to the participants of the march on Washington in August 1963.

OPPOSITE: The grounds of the Washington Monument were packed for Dr King's address in August 1963.

ABOVE: A broad collection of labor and religious groups were represented in the 1963 March on Washington.

RIGHT: Dr King eagerly shakes hands with marchers.

OPPOSITE TOP: A large billboard in Selma, Alabama, portrayed Dr King as a communist.

OPPOSITE BOTTOM RIGHT: Dr King exits Hoover's office in December 1964. King had requested the meeting in an attempt to cool the personal feud between the director and himself.

OPPOSITE BOTTOM LEFT: The FBI felt that New York lawyer Samuel R Pierce Jr was the 'right kind' of black leader to promote.

BELOW: President Kennedy confers with Hoover in a White House meeting.

brother in the White House with a cover note saying, 'I thought you would be interested in the attached memorandum.'

Robert Kennedy had previously rejected Hoover's recommendations to tap King's own telephone for two reasons: because the minister was traveling almost constantly, a tap on his home phone would be likely to yield little useful information, and there was a greak risk of embarrassment and political fallout if it became known the government was spying on the civil rights leader. But in October 1963, Hoover pressed for approval of complete electronic surveillance of King on the basis of Levison's alleged continuing connection with the Communist Party. The attorney general approved 'technical coverage on King' on a trial basis.

In early November 1963, wiretaps were installed on four telephone lines at the SCLC headquarters in Atlanta and on King's private line in his Atlanta home. The phone taps produced more details of King's personal life and sexual activities, and the bureau's interest shifted from King's alleged communist link to his morality.

'King must, at some propitious point in the future, be revealed to the people of this country and to his Negro followers as being what he actually is – a fraud, demagogue and moral scoundrel,' wrote Assistant FBI Director William Sullivan in an 8 January 1964 memorandum.

Sullivan's memo added that, because the exposure of King could leave the nation's blacks 'without a national leader of sufficiently compelling personality to steer them in the proper direction,' steps should be taken to find 'the right kind of a national Negro leader [to] be gradually developed so as to overshadow Dr King and be in the position to assure the role of leadership of the Negro people when King has been completely discredited.' Sullivan suggested that New York lawyer Samuel R Pierce Jr was the 'right kind' of black leader to promote;

Hoover gave Sullivan his OK to begin quietly promoting Pierce toward the national leadership.

By November 1964, Hoover's opinion of King had reached the point that the director was no longer willing to let King's criticism of the FBI's civil rights record go unanswered. In denying a report that King had charged that Southern-born law enforcement officers, FBI agents included, did not vigorously protect civil rights demonstrators, Hoover told reporters, 'In view of King's attitude and his continued criticism of the FBI on this point, I consider King to be the most notorious liar in the country.' The following day, King issued this startled response to the director's remark: 'I cannot

ABOVE: Three stalwarts of the civil rights movement, the Rev Fred Shuttlesworth, the Rev Ralph Abernathy and Dr King, walk to a press conference in Birmingham in May 1963.

RIGHT: Coretta Scott King, widow of Dr King, addresses a peace rally in Washington in 1969.

OPPOSITE: President Kennedy in Massachusetts during a television interview. In July 1963 he warned Dr King to drop his associations with Stanley David Levison and Jack O'Dell, as their past communist ties could hinder the administration's civil rights efforts.

conceive of Mr Hoover making a statement like this without being under extreme pressure. He has apparently faltered under the awesome burden, complexities and responsibilities of his office. I have nothing but sympathy for this man who has served his country so well.'

A week later, King, along with SCLC leaders Ralph Abernathy and Andrew Young, went to Hoover's office for an hour-long meeting with the director. After Abernathy made a few favorable comments about the bureau, King made a brief statement to the effect that his remarks about the role of the FBI in civil rights cases was misquoted in the press. Hoover devoted the remaining 50 minutes of the meeting to a lecture extolling the bureau's strenuous and effective efforts in civil rights cases.

Days before the meeting, Assistant Director William Sullivan prepared a collection of 'highlights' of King's sexual exploits from the taped phone conversations and mailed the tape, along with a vaguely threatening, anonymous letter purportedly from a black person, to King. It was King's wife, Coretta,

RIGHT: Attorney General Ramsey Clark ordered an immediate investigation into King's assassination.

who opened the package weeks later. The bureau also tried unsuccessfully to leak portions of the wiretap transcripts to several reporters, and shared details of the conversations with members of the Baptist clergy and a number of conservative politicians.

Despite efforts to discredit him, King remained atop the leadership of the civil rights movement until his assassination in Memphis, Tennessee, on 4 April 1968. At word of the slaying, Attorney General Ramsey Clark ordered the FBI to conduct an immediate inquiry to determine whether any federal law had been violated. On 17 April the FBI issued a wanted poster for James Earl Ray, charged with 'conspiring to interfere with the constitutional right of a citizen' in the King shooting. Ray was arrested in London, England, two months later and returned to

BELOW: Dr King receives the Nobel Peace Prize in December 1964.

LEFT: Dr King and aides, including Jesse Jackson to his left, standing on a motel balcony in Memphis just moments before King was shot and killed in April 1968.

BELOW: Mrs King and her children at her husband's casket.

the United States for trial. On 10 March 1969, Ray pleaded guilty to King's murder and was sentenced to 99 years in the Tennessee state prison.

If blacks were critical of the bureau's civil rights record, the FBI also engendered hostility on the part of Southern whites, who fumed at what they saw as encroachment of a federal police state into their regional traditions. Agents were often assaulted by whites as they investigated civil rights cases. Typical was the case of a Georgia farmer who in 1962 threw a punch and smashed the glasses of FBI Agent Paul Mohr, who was investigating a fire at a black church. Four months later, the Justice Department took evidence of assault on a federal officer to a federal grand jury, but the jurors announced no true bill.

Also typical was the verbal punch thrown by an editorial in the Roanoke (Virginia) *World-News* when four white men were arrested following the FBI investigation of the burning of the black I Hope Baptist Church in Terrell County, Georgia, in September 1962:

> It is highly regrettable . . . that the apprehensions came through investigations of FBI men and not by local officials. . . . There never was any indication that a federal statute had been violated, but there has been an increasing use of the FBI by the Justice Department. . . . Each such incursion by federal operatives is bound to help whittle away the authority of state and local government. Its constant repetition can lead eventually to nationwide

ABOVE: James Earl Ray (center), Dr King's alleged assassin, at a hearing in Nashville in 1969.

RIGHT: Klansmen protest the 1964 Civil Rights Bill in Jacksonville, Florida.

federal policing . . . not in keeping with constitutional intent. We rejoice that the arsonists have been brought to justice, but we only can regret the implications of federal intervention without proper legal authority.

J Edgar Hoover called the editorial 'ill-informed and misleading,' noting that there was 'strong reason to believe that the [I Hope] church had been set on fire in an effort to intimidate Negroes from registering to vote.' Local churches were commonly used for voter registration meetings in rural black communities in the South. 'FBI agents who arrived at the flaming church shortly after 2 AM concluded quite logically that they should immediately start investigating,' Hoover said. The FBI later withdrew from the I Hope Baptist Church case and turned all its evidence over to state authorities. Three of the defendants drew seven-year prison terms. The fourth, a teenager, was put on probation.

'The FBI is charged with the responsibility of investigating alleged violations of civil rights. This, of course, has never been a popular role. We are criticized on the one hand by those who cry "national police" and usurpation of functions rightfully reserved to the states. On the other hand, we are attacked by those who say we have hedged on civil rights matters involving members of law enforcement agencies,' Hoover observed.

On 22 November 1963, the United States was dealt a staggering blow. Despite the efforts of its top police and security forces, the government's chief executive, parading confidently through an American city, was picked off by a sniper. In its grief, the nation groped for answers, not only to the question 'why?' but to the more practical question of how an assassin's bullet could have found its way to the president. In the post-mortem, the FBI received a share of the blame for failing to act on information in its file on Lee Harvey Oswald.

Lee Harvey Oswald, a surly malcontent, ex-Marine and self-styled Marxist, drew the attention of the FBI when he returned from Moscow to the United States in June 1962 after aborting his 1959 defection to the Soviet Union. Disillusioned with life in communist Russia, Oswald had returned to America with his Russian wife and moved to a Dallas suburb in the fall of 1963.

By 4 November of that year, Special Agent James P Hosty Jr, a member of the FBI's 75-man Dallas office, knew Oswald, 24, was working at the Texas School Book Depository at the corner of Houston and Elm streets, and that the building commanded a

ABOVE: Horace Barnette, 22, one of 21 people charged in the 1963 murder of three civil rights workers in Mississippi.

LEFT: Lee Harvey Oswald, the alleged assassin of President Kennedy.

Гостиница „МЕТРОПОЛЬ"
г. Москва

I, Lee Harvey Oswald do hereby request that my present citizenship in the United States of America, be revoked.

I have entered the Soviet Union for the express purpose of applying for citizenship in the Soviet Union, through the means of naturalization.

My request for citizenship is now pending before the Supreme Soviet of the U.S.S.R.

I take these steps for political reasons.

My request for the revoking of my American citizenship is made only after the longest and most serious considerations.

I affirm that my allegiance is to the Union of Soviet Socialist Republics.

ABOVE: A note from Oswald to the US Embassy in Moscow asking that his American citizenship be revoked.

OPPOSITE: The Texas School Book Depository from which Oswald allegedly fired the shots that killed President Kennedy.

view of President John F Kennedy's motorcade route set for 22 November. Although Hosty had a file on Oswald, the man was not under active FBI surveillance. And, because months of checking had given the bureau no reason to believe he was a spy, saboteur or potential assassin, Oswald's name did not appear on the 'risk' list that the FBI handed over to the Secret Service in preparation for Kennedy's Dallas trip. As a result, the Secret Service did not search the book warehouse, where Oswald had built a sniper's nest at a sixth-floor window that looked out on Dealy Plaza.

LEFT AND BELOW: The
Kennedys arrive to
enthusiastic crowds at
Love Field in Dallas on
22 November 1963.

OPPOSITE: The President's
motorcade in nearby Fort
Worth.

RIGHT: President Kennedy riding in his motorcade approximately one minute before he was shot and killed.

ABOVE: In the moments after the shooting, President Kennedy slumps and Mrs Kennedy rises in her seat as a Secret Service agent rides the bumper.

His perch was grimly effective. President John Fitzgerald Kennedy was dead of a bullet wound in the head at 1 PM, less than half an hour after his open car had passed the window. At 7:25 PM, President Lyndon B Johnson, who had been sworn in aboard Air Force One at Dallas Love Field before flying to Washington, phoned J Edgar Hoover and ordered a full investigation of the assassination. Hoover immediately dispatched a special assistant and 30 agents to Dallas. Ironically, Attorney General Robert Kennedy first heard about his brother's death through a curt call from Hoover. The hostility between the two men had long been apparent. Although Robert Kennedy would continue to head the Justice Department for ten more months, he never spoke with Hoover after 22 November.

Investigating the killing of Kennedy was legally within the jurisdiction of state law enforcement officials in Texas. But Hoover's men actively assisted detectives in Dallas from the start, as well as probing for the possibility of a murder conspiracy.

Hours after the assassination, FBI agents swarmed New Orleans to piece together Oswald's activities during his 20 weeks there just prior to the assassination. Investigators learned Oswald had been active in a pro-Castro group called the Fair Play for Cuba Committee in New Orleans. An examination of his correspondence with the group indicated Oswald had initiated his association with Fair Play and had launched a New Orleans chapter of the group without approval of organization officials. Checking the records of a public library six blocks from Oswald's New Orleans apartment, investigators discovered that the self-described Marxist had, in the weeks before the assassination, checked out a biography of John

Kennedy and a chronicle of the assassination of Senator Huey P Long, as well as four Ian Fleming spy novels and several books about communism.

By 23 November FBI agents assisting Dallas police had identified Oswald's handwriting on the order form with which he had purchased a 1938 model Italian-made 6.5mm Mannlicher-Carcano rifle from the Chicago mail order house of Klein's Sporting Goods. Oswald paid $12.78 for the rifle, which was delivered on 20 March 1963 to a Dallas post office box Oswald had rented under the name 'A Hidell.'

Eighty minutes after Kennedy was shot, Oswald was arrested in a Dallas movie theater three miles from the book warehouse. A half hour earlier, Oswald had shot and killed Dallas patrolman J D Tippit, who had tried to stop and question him. Justice Department laboratory technicians in

ABOVE: The swearing in of President Lyndon Johnson on board Air Force One after the Kennedy shooting.

LEFT: The assassination investigation turned up this photograph of Oswald handing out Fair Play for Cuba handbills.

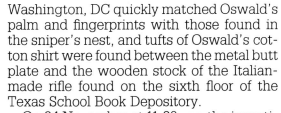

Washington, DC quickly matched Oswald's palm and fingerprints with those found in the sniper's nest, and tufts of Oswald's cotton shirt were found between the metal butt plate and the wooden stock of the Italian-made rifle found on the sixth floor of the Texas School Book Depository.

On 24 November at 11:20 AM, the investigation took a stunning turn. Oswald was shot to death in the basement of the Dallas city jail as officers were moving him to an armored car for transport to a county jail. Jack Rubenstein, known as Jack Ruby, a Dallas nightclub owner, lunged from a pack of reporters watching the transfer, pointed a revolver and fired one fatal shot into Oswald's abdomen. A numbed nation watched the shooting on live television. President Johnson immediately ordered that the FBI probe be intensified and expanded to include possible connections between Oswald and Ruby.

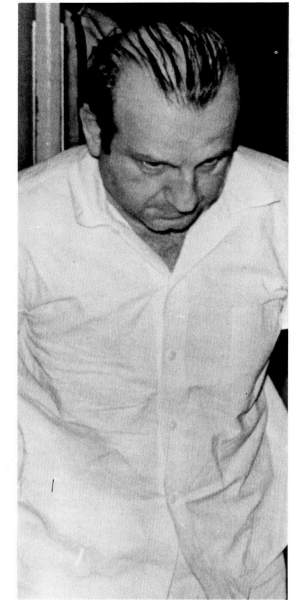

RIGHT: The honor guard brings JFK's casket into the White House on 23 November 1963.

OPPOSITE TOP: Police escort Oswald during his transfer from the Dallas city prison to the county jail just moments before he is shot and killed.

OPPOSITE BOTTOM LEFT: A Dallas policeman holds the weapon used to shoot JFK.

OPPOSITE BOTTOM RIGHT: Jack Ruby in custody shortly after being charged with murdering Oswald.

BELOW: Robert and Ted Kennedy escorting Jacqueline Kennedy in JFK's funeral procession.

On 10 December the FBI handed its findings to the special commission headed by US Supreme Court Chief Justice Earl Warren. The bureau's report concluded that Oswald was, beyond doubt, Kennedy's assassin. The report further stated that Oswald had apparently acted alone from his sniper's perch on the sixth floor of the book warehouse. The FBI also concluded there was no prior connection between Oswald and Jack Ruby. The Warren Commission later reported that the FBI took 'an unduly restrictive view' of its responsibility to share information on Lee Harvey Oswald with the Secret Service or Dallas Police Department before JFK's fateful Texas trip. That criticism drew a sharp response from Hoover, who called it 'unwarranted, untrue and a classic example of Monday-morning quarterbacking.'

Hoover denied the existence of any friction between his agency and the Secret Service or Central Intelligence Agency. 'Such rumors are strictly poppycock since the FBI has always had the very best of relationships with both organizations.' So good was

ABOVE: In 1977, the FBI made public masses of information from its investigation of the president's assassination 14 years earlier.

OPPOSITE: The Honorable Earl Warren, Chief Justice of the Supreme Court, headed the commission investigating the president's murder.

his relationship with the Secret Service, in fact, that after the Warren Commission criticism, Hoover's agency started flooding the agency with the names of potential assassins at the rate of 8000 a year. In his own commission testimony, Hoover had said this would create an excessive burden on those charged with the president's security. Indeed, one year after the assassination, the Secret Service was obliged to hire 75 new agents and re-equip its offices to accomodate the added caseload.

The assassination also led to a law change. On 28 August 1965, the FBI was given specific responsibilities for investigating the killing, assault or kidnaping of the president, vice president and certain other federal government officials.

At the same time as the FBI was struggling with civil rights cases and the Kennedy assassination probe, it also began increasing its efforts at battling organized crime. The catalyst for the new emphasis came from stunning testimony by a former member of La Costa Nostra (the name

— THE FAMILY THAT "PREYS" TOGETHER —

Hoover liked to use in referring to the Mafia) and from law changes that gave FBI agents new investigative powers.

Attorney General Robert Kennedy and others had charged more than once that Hoover was ignoring the rise of the Mafia in America. For years Hoover denied, at least publicly, that any such organization even existed; then he simply pointed out that his agents did not have the authority to investigate most of the Mafia's alleged crimes because they did not involve the violation of federal laws. History reveals, however, that

as early as the 1940s the FBI had investigated certain segments of organized crime. In 1964, the President's Commission on Law Enforcement and the Administration of Justice reported, 'To date, only the Federal Bureau of Investigation has been able to document fully the national scope of these groups.'

Then Joseph Valachi brought La Costa Nostra to the American public in dramatic fashion. Valachi belonged to the Mafia for 30 years before he was convicted of drug violations and sent to the federal penitentiary in

Atlanta in the early 1960s. After his sentencing, the word went out among 'Family' members that Valachi had talked too much during his trial. Valachi believed he was slated for 'elimination.' Paranoid because of the belief that a fellow inmate was his appointed assassin, Valachi killed the man in prison. Valachi was sentenced to life in prison for the killing, and still carried a $100,000 bounty on his head.

Valachi turned informant and talked to the FBI, the Organized Crime section of the Justice Department and the Senate Permanent Subcommittee on Investigations. What he had to tell was sensational. No one before had outlined the workings of the mob in America. Valachi provided solid proof that La Cosa Nostra had, indeed, established a strong organization in the United States.

By the time Valachi testified, the FBI had, or was about to get, new authority that would allow the agency to delve into more of the Mafia's activities. In 1961, four new laws made federal crimes of transporting wagering paraphernalia across state lines, transmitting betting information between states, destroying property moving in inter-

state or international commerce, and traveling between states to aid racketeering. The National Firearms Act, the Fugitive Act and other laws were amended and strengthened for the fight against crime syndicates. Other federal statutes passed in the next few years, such as one dealing with schemes to influence the outcome of sporting events through bribery, also expanded the scope of the FBI.

The actions of antiwar and other protest groups in the late 1960s planted the seeds for the controversy that would grow to maturity in the 1970s: the revelation that Hoover had directed his agents to conduct intensive counterintelligence operations against New Left organizations, black militants and civil rights groups. While some of these organizations obviously posed the real threat of violence – most notably the Weathermen – many other targeted groups were simply exercising First Amendment rights. In the view of many civil libertarians, overzealous justice was again tromping on the toes of American liberty.

Near the end of Hoover's reign, more and more people were calling for him to step down. It had been rumored in 1964 that Pre-

ABOVE: Supporters of the Vietnam War carrying anti-communist placards.

OPPOSITE TOP: Underworld figure Joseph Valachi takes an oath before testifying about organized crime activity before a Senate subcommittee in September 1963.

OPPOSITE BOTTOM: President Richard M Nixon signing legislation in 1970 to set up a council to establish a national campaign against organized crime.

sident Lyndon Johnson planned to force Hoover to accept mandatory retirement. Instead, Johnson exempted Hoover from compulsory retirement. In the early 1970s, when public sentiment to find a new FBI chief was even stronger, President Richard Nixon called Hoover to a luncheon meeting with the intention of telling him it was time for him to step down. Nixon backed out at the last minute and Hoover stayed on.

At the end, America's preeminent G-man had outlived his legend. Washington buzzed louder and longer of the FBI's preoccupation with the digging of political dirt. 'I think people felt he had a dossier on Saint Peter,' quipped one congressional staffer. Hoover served under every US president from Calvin Coolidge to Richard Nixon, and, with 48 years at the top of the country's top law enforcement agency, he had held more power longer than any person in American history. Many had come to fear that Hoover was directing that power toward his rivals – real or imagined – in the government, rather than focusing on organized crime, drug trafficking and espionage. But his power had become such that even presidents were hesitant to challenge him.

Ironically, it was on the eve of what was to become the nation's most celebrated political scandal, the stuff on which Hoover had come to thrive, that the director re-

'THE MORE THINGS CHANGE THE MORE THEY STAY THE SAME'

linquished the bureau by the only means possible: death. Hoover seemed healthy enough to those who saw him at his favorite Saturday haunt, the $2 window at Pimlico racetrack, on 29 April 1972. The following Monday, he was at his usual table at the Mayflower Hotel, having his usual lunch with Associate FBI Director and long-time companion Clyde Tolson. His work sche-

ABOVE: One of the last photos taken of Hoover, in February 1972.

dule that day was full but routine. There was nothing to hint that J Edgar Hoover, 77, would be dead by Tuesday morning, 2 May 1972. He died in his bed at his neo-Georgian house at the edge of Washington's Rock Creek Park, apparently of heart disease complicated by high blood pressure.

An estimated 25,000 mourners filed past Hoover's casket as it lay in state in the Capitol rotunda. It was the first time an appointed government official had been so honored. President Nixon, an admirer of Hoover since the Alger Hiss case, delivered the director's eulogy at the funeral service at Washington's National Presbyterian Church. 'The United States is a better country because this good man lived his long life among us,' Nixon said. The American flag from the casket was folded and presented to Clyde Tolson, who succeeded Hoover for two days and then retired.

Six weeks after Hoover's death, burglars working for President Nixon's re-election committee were arrested while attempting to replace a faulty telephone tap in the Democratic National Committee headquarters at the swank Watergate office complex in Washington. One can only imagine what Hoover would have made of the intrigue that ensued.

CHAPTER SEVEN

THE BUREAU AFTER HOOVER

OPPOSITE: President Nixon and his wife during a ticker-tape parade.

BELOW: Following Hoover's death, Nixon appointed L Patrick Gray III (shown here) as interim director of the FBI.

J Edgar Hoover had hardly been buried when it became apparent that the naming of his replacement was going to result in a powerful internal struggle among top FBI aides. But the struggle had barely begun when President Richard M Nixon put a stop to it by naming an old friend and confidant, L Patrick Gray III, to the director's post on an interim basis.

There were questions and doubts about Gray from the beginning. He had no law enforcement experience and, unlike Hoover in the beginning, he had heavy political connections to the president. Those political entanglements would be his downfall within a year. But first, Gray would start making some badly needed changes within the bureau.

Gray was a retired Navy captain and a lawyer who had served eight years as a special assistant to then-Vice President Richard Nixon during President Dwight D Eisenhower's administration. Gray was serving as an assistant attorney general in charge of the Justice Department's Civil Division when he was asked to step into Hoover's shoes. Because his appointment as head of the FBI was not permanent at that point, Gray also remained at his post in the Civil Division at Justice, although his pending nomination to be deputy attorney general was withdrawn.

It was clear that if Nixon were re-elected in 1972 he intended to nominate Acting Director Gray for the regular appointment. Only three months after being named interim head of the bureau, it was quite clear that Gray, although a hard-line law and order man, was taking the agency in some new directions. He effected an immediate improvement in agent morale by relaxing Hoover's strict dress and hair codes, and by eliminating some of the petty rules that Hoover used to keep his men in perpetual fear. Gray made it clear that he did not expect to see agents looking like street bums, but he also said he did not see how some of the old rules had anything to do with an agent's job performance. 'I don't judge the performance of a person on the basis of the color of his shirt, for example,' he told a reporter. 'I don't judge a person on the type of suit he wears, or the length of his hair, or his hair style.'

And no longer would the bureau include only G-Men; women would join the ranks of special agents. Hoover had adamantly refused to allow women to be special agents, saying that tracking down criminals was too dangerous for them. He ignored the Equal Employment Opportunity Act that, by most

interpretations, mandated his hiring of females. Gray quickly swore in the first two 'G-Women' in the FBI's history: one a former nun, the other a former officer in the United States Marine Corps.

In his last decade, Hoover had slowly, grudgingly begun hiring more members of racial and ethnic minorities into the ranks of the bureau. Gray attempted to speed up that process by establishing a new office to recruit more blacks, Hispanics, Native Americans and Asian-Americans. By the early 1980s, building on what Gray had started, the bureau had more than 350 female agents and more than 200 blacks. Only a minority of the new agents had been either lawyers or accountants; Hoover insisted on hiring only accountants or lawyers as agents during most of his tenure.

Gray said he considered crime statistics an important tool for the bureau, but he softened the bureau's emphasis on them.

Critics had long complained that Hoover could and did use statistics to shape the public image of the agency. Gray said he intended to switch the bureau's emphasis away from statistics-building cases and focus more resources on the bigger, more difficult problems of organized crime, drug abuse and white collar crime. That sort of work may not generate the kind of flashy statistics that Hoover relished, but the switch in resources was long overdue.

Despite his efforts at reform, Gray would ultimately hurt more than help the FBI's image. The acting director (and, to a lesser extent, the agency in his charge) would buckle under the weight of the heaviest government scandal in the history of the United States. L Patrick Gray was among those Nixon loyalists whose reputations would soon lie mangled beneath the rubble of Watergate.

'A third-rate burglary' is how President

OPPOSITE TOP: Gray with his 15 assistant directors in the renovated FBI offices in May 1972.

OPPOSITE BOTTOM: Five women were sworn in as the first female agents of the US Secret Service in December 1971.

BELOW: An aerial view of the Watergate complex in Washington, DC.

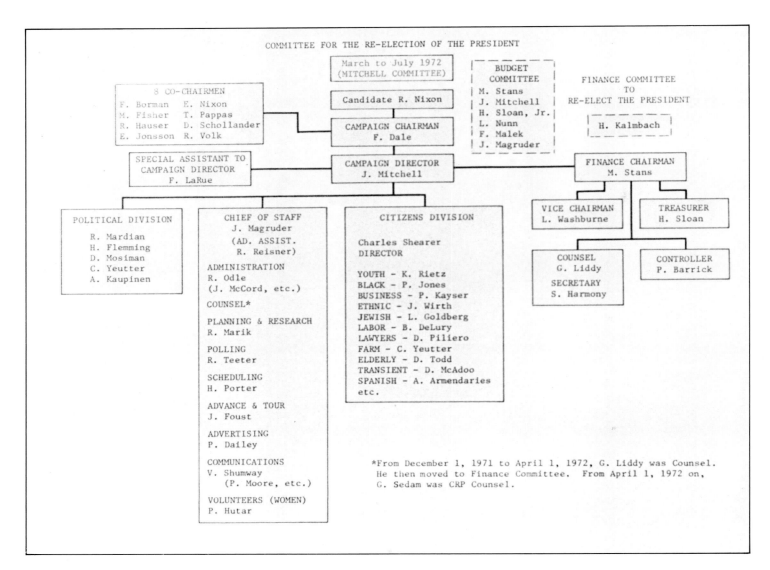

COMMITTEE FOR THE RE-ELECTION OF THE PRESIDENT

March to July 1972
(MITCHELL COMMITTEE)

Candidate R. Nixon

BUDGET COMMITTEE
M. Stans
J. Mitchell
H. Sloan, Jr.
L. Nunn
F. Malek
J. Magruder

FINANCE COMMITTEE
TO
RE-ELECT THE PRESIDENT

H. Kalmbach

8 CO-CHAIRMEN
F. Borman   E. Nixon
M. Fisher   T. Pappas
R. Hauser   D. Schollander
E. Jonsson   R. Volk

CAMPAIGN CHAIRMAN
F. Dale

SPECIAL ASSISTANT TO
CAMPAIGN DIRECTOR
F. LaRue

CAMPAIGN DIRECTOR
J. Mitchell

FINANCE CHAIRMAN
M. Stans

POLITICAL DIVISION
R. Mardian
H. Flemming
D. Mosiman
C. Yeutter
A. Kaupinen

CHIEF OF STAFF
J. Magruder
(AD. ASSIST.
R. Reisner)

ADMINISTRATION
R. Odle
(J. McCord, etc.)

COUNSEL*

PLANNING & RESEARCH
R. Marik

POLLING
R. Teeter

SCHEDULING
H. Porter

ADVANCE & TOUR
J. Foust

ADVERTISING
P. Dailey

COMMUNICATIONS
V. Shumway
(P. Moore, etc.)

VOLUNTEERS (WOMEN)
P. Hutar

CITIZENS DIVISION

Charles Shearer
DIRECTOR

YOUTH - K. Rietz
BLACK - P. Jones
BUSINESS - P. Kayser
ETHNIC - J. Wirth
JEWISH - L. Goldberg
LABOR - B. DeLury
LAWYERS - D. Piliero
FARM - C. Yeutter
ELDERLY - D. Todd
TRANSIENT - D. McAdoo
SPANISH - A. Armendaries
etc.

VICE CHAIRMAN
L. Washburne

TREASURER
H. Sloan

COUNSEL
G. Liddy

SECRETARY
S. Harmony

CONTROLLER
P. Barrick

*From December 1, 1971 to April 1, 1972, G. Liddy was Counsel.
He then moved to Finance Committee. From April 1, 1972 on,
G. Sedam was CRP Counsel.

ABOVE: This organizational chart from the Nixon campaign became a blueprint for Watergate conspiracy.

OPPOSITE: Former Attorney General John Mitchell leaves federal court in New York in 1973 after pleading innocent to perjury and conspiracy charges.

Nixon described the 17 June 1972 break-in of the Democratic National Committee headquarters at the Watergate office complex in Washington, DC. The men were attempting to replace a faulty telephone bug when they were caught. At first, it seemed the crime was limited to the five men arrested inside the office and two accomplices stationed nearby. But a conspiracy of silence by the burglars was broken in March 1973, when one of the men linked the break-in to the head of President Nixon's re-election committee, former Attorney General John Mitchell. Acting FBI Director Gray did his part in unraveling the plot, and ruining his own reputation, when he went before Congress seeking confirmation as full-time head of the detective agency.

Gray was exposed as an inept administrator and a dupe of the White House staff when he appeared before the Senate Judiciary Committee in March 1973. The Senate Select Committee on Watergate had not yet started its televised hearings, and there was not yet a special prosecutor assigned to the case when Gray went before the Judiciary

Committee for hearings on his nomination to become permanent FBI director. Although the press, particularly the *Washington Post*, had been chipping away at the protective stone wall around President Nixon, the wall was still standing when Gray faced the committee.

During Gray's testimony, the committee learned that the Justice Department had put restraints on the FBI's Watergate investigation (and that Gray was unperturbed by the fetters.) Attorneys for the Committee to Re-Elect the President (CREEP) had been allowed to sit in during FBI agents' interviews with CREEP staffers. Gray testified that he had discussed the progress of the investigation with White House aide John Erlichman and John Dean, counsel to the president. Gray testified that he also made written reports on the probe to Dean, channeling the communications through Attorney General Richard Kleindienst.

Dean, who had yet to become a central figure in the Watergate drama, was ostensibly conducting his own investigation of the Watergate break-in for President Nixon.

ABOVE: Former top Nixon White House aide John Erlichman speaks with reporters in May 1973.

RIGHT: Attorney General Richard Kleindienst, with a large portrait of President Nixon in the background, addresses 'Lawyers for the President' in May 1972 in Miami Beach.

OPPOSITE TOP: John Dean III, the fired White House counsel, begins his testimony before the Senate Watergate committee in June 1973.

OPPOSITE BOTTOM: Former FBI Director Gray and his wife leave federal court in Washington in April 1978 after he pleaded innocent to illegal wiretapping charges.

Gray, therefore, was correct in sharing raw investigative data, Nixon argued. (Dean would later tell the Senate Watergate Committee that he had actually been attempting to cover up the involvement of the president and his staff.)

Dean, alarmed by Gray's testimony before the Judiciary Committee, feared the committee might hold back Gray's confirmation until hearing testimony from members of the president's staff, which would jeopardize the cover-up. Because Nixon had already decided to claim executive privilege to prevent his aides from testifying, Gray could be 'left hanging,' Dean observed. 'Well, I think we ought to let him hang there,' Erlichman replied. 'Let him twist slowly, slowly in the wind.'

Gray hung and twisted slowly in the wind of public shame until April 1973, when Nixon withdrew his nomination as FBI director; Gray resigned as interim director of the bureau soon after. Four months later, Gray told the Senate Watergate Committee that he, while acting director, had destroyed secret bureau files at the behest of Dean and Erlichman, and then had lied about his actions.

Into the troubled void left by Gray stepped Clarence M Kelley, chief of the Kansas City Police Department, a former FBI

agent and one of 27 finalists for the director's post. It was to be Kelley's second stint with the FBI. He had been with the agency for 21 years, the last few as head of the FBI's Memphis office. He had left that job in 1961 to take over as chief of the Kansas City police force, and was credited with introducing innovative programs and increasing the hiring of black officers.

Kelley tried to salvage the bureau's investigative integrity by offering complete cooperation to Watergate Special Prosecutor Leon Jaworski in his efforts to track the White House involvement in the Watergate break-in and subsequent cover-up. Tiptoeing along the fine line between loyalty to the embattled president and faithfulness to his duty to his country, Kelley led the bureau into the fray in a manner that later drew the praise of Jaworski. 'Kelley . . . did much to restore public confidence in the FBI,' Jaworski wrote in his 1976 book *The Right and The Power*. The special prosecutor said Kelley was aggressive and professional in assisting with the investigation of the mysterious 18-and-a-half-minute gap in conversations tape-recorded in the Oval Office during crucial talks between Nixon and his aides during the Watergate cover-up.

Kelley would spend much of his nearly four years as FBI director fielding questions

LEFT: Watergate prosecutor Leon Jaworski in 1974.

OPPOSITE TOP: Clarence Kelley is sworn in as FBI director in July 1973.

OPPOSITE BOTTOM: Senator Howard Baker of Tennessee, left, and Senator Sam Ervin of North Carolina, right, during the Watergate hearings.

BELOW: Television played a large role in Watergate.

Drawing by Handelsman; ©1967 The New Yorker Magazine, Inc.
"If you didn't sneeze and I didn't sneeze, then the F.B.I. must have sneezed."

about past abuses of the bureau and trying to reassure the American people that things had changed. Kelley was kept on the defensive by revelations that struck at the heart of the liberty-justice dilemma.

Beginning after Hoover's death, facts and rumors emerged that gave breath to the old fear of the FBI as a secret police force. It was learned that Hoover had, despite his repeated denials, gathered secret files on politicians and other public figures, and had used the files to discredit his opponents. Reports revealed that the Hoover files had also been used to discredit the enemies of presidents Lyndon Johnson and Richard Nixon.

Attorney General Edward H Levi confirmed the existence of the secret files in 1975. They included unproven allegations about the morals and drinking habits of select congressmen and other prominent figures. Levi also acknowledged that over the years the FBI's counterintelligence unit had released derogatory information about persons considered extremists in an effort to

discredit them. The revelations left an ugly smear on the reputation of the nation's pre-eminent detective agency.

Throughout the 1970s, evidence emerged that the FBI had participated in 'black-bag' jobs and illegal wiretaps, harassed the Reverend Martin Luther King Jr and attempted to undermine anti-Vietnam War protesters. There was evidence, too, that Hoover sometimes used secret information to intimidate or blackmail people. When he picked up a rumor or tip about an opponent's indiscretion, Hoover would sometimes leak the information to the press. Other times he would keep the tidbit out of the papers, but notify the offending person by courier that the FBI knew of his secret. Implied with the message was the threat that the director would leak the information if the person did not cooperate.

Kelley struggled with these revelations as he attempted to steer an agency that, by the 1970s, had grown to more than 20,000 employees working in 185 separate investigative specialties ranging from domestic

security to looking into the sale of switch-blade knives. After leaving the bureau, Kelley would complain that he was forced to spend too much time fending off criticism of his predecessors and was left too little time for his real work. He said the agency's accomplishments during his watch were largely ignored in the rush to wallow in the bad news of the Hoover years.

Bad news of another sort struck on 26 June 1975 when two agents were shot to death on the Oglala Sioux Indian Reservation near Pine Ridge, South Dakota as they approached a house known to be occupied by supporters of the American Indian Movement, a militant organization. Pine Ridge is near Wounded Knee, and both areas had been torn by dissension and violence for at least two years. Oglala Sioux Indians had, at various times, taken over sections of the reservation to protest government treatment. Indians had been killed, and US marshals were wounded in shootouts.

Reports on the killings differed. One bureau spokesman said that agents Jack R

ABOVE: American Indian Movement leaders Russell Means, left, and Dennis Banks, right, at a rally in Minnesota in 1974.

OPPOSITE TOP: Attorney General Edward Levi, right, disclosed to a House subcommittee in 1975 that J Edgar Hoover had compiled derogatory information on several presidents and other public figures. Also pictured is FBI Director Clarence Kelley.

OPPOSITE BOTTOM: Cartoon poking fun at federal eavesdropping.

Coler and Ronald A Williams went to the house to serve warrants on four men suspected of holding visitors to the reservation against their will. But they had no warrants, and some of the Indians tried to claim they were killed by other police officers. The agents were hit by rifle fire as they got out of their car. They were unable to radio for help, and a gun battle ensued. Coler and Williams died, and an Indian also was killed. The FBI immediately flooded the reservation with 300 agents looking for clues. One FBI helicopter had to land after being fired on. Months later, four Indians were indicted for the murders and Leonard Peltier, an Indian activist, was convicted.

The Patty Hearst kidnaping in 1974 was to be both an embarrassment and a triumph for the FBI. From the time she was abducted from her Berkeley, California apartment by members of the Symbionese Liberation Army, the public in general expected the FBI to find her quickly. But underground organizations did not follow common criminal routines, which made them harder to locate. And no one knew that Patty Hearst had quickly become what she later described as an 'urban guerrilla,' essentially becoming a cooperative member of the group. For various reasons, she did not want to be found. More than one police official used the old cliche 'hunting for a needle in a haystack' to describe the search for Hearst. Nonetheless, the FBI came under a lot of fire when it took agents 19 months to find Hearst, who by then was calling herself Tania. It also got some well-deserved plaudits for the detective work that led to her capture.

Hearst was kidnaped by Donald DeFreeze, the leader of the SLA, Willie Wolfe and Nancy Ling Perry. Although she was not physically harmed or sexually assaulted, DeFreeze kept up a constant stream of verbal abuse. The kidnapers demanded a huge ransom of $10 million. It wasn't long before Hearst, convinced that her parents didn't really care about her, didn't want to go back.

Randolph Hearst, the publisher and Patty's father, liked the FBI agents in his area, but he had little faith they would find her on their own. So while the FBI was investigating, he also put out his own offers and made his own efforts at locating her. He went through a succession of useless ideas and con men who tried to separate him from a fraction of his huge fortune.

By September 1974, some SLA members, including DeFreeze, were dead in a shootout with Los Angeles police. By then, Patty had moved with other members to Penn-

ABOVE: FBI Director Kelley arrives at the Federal Court in Iowa in 1976 to testify at the trial of two American Indians accused in the murder of two FBI agents.

LEFT: Newspaper heiress Patty Hearst as a member of the Symbionese Liberation Army.

OPPOSITE: Leonard Peltier, American Indian Movement leader, being deported by Canadian authorities in 1975 to face charges connected to the murder of two FBI agents.

ABOVE: Once considered a victim, Patty Hearst soon appeared on the FBI's wanted list.

LEFT: Publisher Randolph Hearst announces in San Francisco in 1974 that $2 million in free food will be distributed to the poor and needy in an effort to obtain the release of Patty Hearst from her kidnapers.

OPPOSITE: The front page of Randolph Hearst's *San Francisco Examiner* headlined the capture of his daughter and SLA fugitives Bill and Emily Harris on 18 September 1975.

Patricia Hearst, arrested in S.F. today

PATTY HEARST, SLA COUPLE CAUGHT HERE

San Francisco Examiner

111th Year   No. 85   ☆☆☆   SU 1-2424   THURSDAY, SEPTEMBER 18, 1975   Daily 20c   FINAL EDITION COMPLETE STOCKS

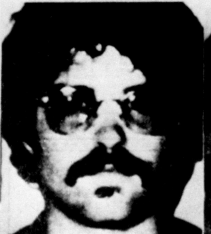 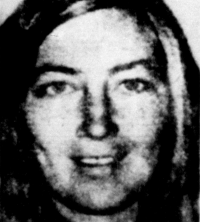

Bill and Emily Harris: Their long flight from the law ended in San Francisco

Four found in S.F. houses —give up

Patricia Hearst and Symbionese Liberation Army fugitives William and Emily Harris were arrested in San Francisco today.

The Harrises were arrested at 1:10 p.m. as they left the apartment they had been living in at 288 Precita in the Bernal Heights Area.

Miss Hearst and another fugitive, Wendy Yoshimura, were arrested at 2:20 p.m. in a house at 625 Morse St. in the outer Q Mission District.

None of the fugitives offered resistance, said FBI Agent in Charge Charles Bates.

None were disguised, Bates said.

Catherine Hearst, mother of Patricia, learned of her daughter's arrest while attending a meeting of the University of California Regents in Los Angeles.

"They found Patty. Thank God she's all right," she said, before catching a plane back to San Francisco.

Miss Hearst's father, Randolph A. Hearst, said he understood his daughter and the Harrises were all in good physical condition. He had no further comment.

Miss Hearst was kidnaped by the Symbionese Liberation Army from her Berkeley apartment Feb. 4, 1974.

Bates said the Harrises were wearing jogging clothes when arrested on the street.

He said Miss Hearst appeared to be in good condition. She was wearing tan slacks, he said.

The investigation leading to the arrest which closed out a year and a half long manhunt began "several days ago," said Bates.

The close of the case was due to "hard work and effort," he said.

He was always certain Miss Hearst and the Harrises would be found and arrested, he said, "It was just a question of when. But no time believed me."

The Harrises were brought to the Federal Building at 1:30 p.m. in separate cars.

William Harris, his hands cuffed in front of him, had a beard and long dark hair.

Emily Harris, her blonde hair cut short, was wearing white tennis shorts and a blouse. Her hands were cuffed behind her

Browning on the pair were

being held on 19 charges involving robbery, kidnap, auto theft and assault with a deadly weapon filed by the Los Angeles District Attorney after they escaped arrest there in 1974.

They also face federal firearms act charges in U.S. District Court.

Bail will probably be set at $500,000 for each Browning said.

The Harrises and Miss Hearst were last known to have been together in a small farmhouse hideout near New Canaan, Pa. last fall.

Their fingerprints were found in the building rented by Mich Scott in the countryside outside of Scranton.

They disappeared together May 16, 1974 after a shootout at a Los Angeles sporting goods store triggered when a clerk saw Harris try to shoplift a pair of socks.

Miss Hearst has been with the SLA members since her Feb. 4 1974 kidnap from her Berkeley apartment.

She was carried screaming into the night by two men and a woman and stuffed into the trunk of a car.

She later announced via tape recordings that she had joined the SLA and adopted the revolutionary name, Tania.

Alameda County District Attorney Lowell Jensen, upon hearing of the arrests, said he has no charges against the Harrises but is contemplating asking the county grand jury to indict them for the kidnaping of Miss Hearst.

Miss Hearst is still wanted on 19 state charges, all but one of which the charges with the Harrises in Los Angeles, and federal bank robbery and firearms violations charges.

The couple was scheduled to appear for a hearing before U.S. Magistrate Owen Woodruff Jr. this afternoon on the question of whether they would be immediately removed from federal jurisdiction to face the Los Angeles charges.

Citizen vigilantes ride in 23 counties

By Larry D. Hatfield

"You know," says a young electrician in Stockton, "a law enforcement agency can't do anything any more without getting in trouble."

In Petaluma, a part-time preacher adds, "If it ever comes to that, we'll have to start taking the people who pervert the law while holding public office, arrest them. They used to hang them."

And in Grass Valley a middle-aged telephone installer adds, "You won't find a single automatic weapon in the bunch, just normal people with weapons of the 20-30s.

These three men, and an untold number of other "average Americans, have a lot in common; they are private citizens, they believe your home is your castle, they tend towards the right, they don't trust the government or its enforcers — and they have guns.

Jim McDaniel, head of the "posse comitatus" (power of the county) in San Joaquin County said the shooting incident occurred "because we haven't had any training among our people. It will not happen again because we are starting a training program. The member who did the shooting which authorities said was accidental, has been suspended because he just overstepped.

A 36-year-old high school educated electrician, McDaniel says state and federal laws "require, not suggest" that every male 18 years old and over "aid and assist in preventing any breach of the

They are also members of citizen vigilante groups that a Justice Department official says are "popping up like pimples" all across the nation.

In California alone, these citizen posses reportedly exist in 23 counties. Estimates of their membership nationwide range from less than 10,000 up to 800,000.

Although they have been active in California for several months, the vigilante groups only recently gained widespread notoriety when one of them, at gunpoint, kept United Farm Workers organizers out of fields in the San Joaquin Valley.

One deputy sheriff was almost shot in the head during one of the tense confrontations at a tomato field near Stockton.

— See Back Page, Col. 1

U.S. narcotics agents linked to murders

By William F. Mooney and William Crawford of 1975 Chicago Daily News

CHICAGO — The Justice Department has uncovered evidence linking Drug Enforcement Administration officials and American hoodlums to murder, blackmail, smuggling, extortion and black marketing drugs and gold.

A special task force appointed by Attorney General Edward Levi found the evidence buried in DEA's own files, but has not turned this information over to the White House Domestic Council headed by Vice President Rockefeller.

DEA, as part of the Justice Department, is under Levi.

The Domestic Council has drafted a White Paper report recommending that DEA continue to be the front line of defense in the heroin war.

The Customs Service, a branch of the Treasury Department, is downgraded and given only a minor role by the Domestic Council.

The White Paper report, several months in the making, was drafted without access to the findings of Levi's task force.

The evidence uncovered in DEA files has been turned over to the criminal division of the Justice Department.

A Justice Department source

— See Back Page, Col. 1

How the CIA and Army lied on Viet Cong

Examiner News Services

WASHINGTON — The United States was caught off guard by the 1968 Tet offensive in South Vietnam because intelligence estimates of the strength of enemy forces were altered to "project an image" of American success, a former CIA official said today.

"Although our aim was to fool the American press, the public and the Congress, we in intelligence succeeded best in fooling ourselves," Samuel Adams, a former CIA analyst, told Congress.

Adams, testifying before the House Intelligence Committee, produced secret cables from Gen. Creighton Abrams, former U.S. commander in Vietnam, and Ellsworth Bunker, former ambassador to Saigon.

Adams said Abrams and Bunker insisted on estimating Viet Cong troop strength at 300,000, despite reports that indicated enemy strength at 600,000.

He said the figures were altered to support their contention that the Viet Cong were demoralized by U.S. military successes.

The misinformation led to U.S. military forces, the Congress and the American public being caught by surprise at the intensity of the Tet offensive Jan. 30, 1968, Adams said.

The two cables produced by

— See Back Page, Col. 5

Quotable

As the administration sees it, things are getting better because they're getting worse slower.

Paul L. Nelson

sylvania, and later returned to San Francisco. On 21 April 1975, five people robbed the Crocker National Bank in Carmichael, California. The FBI identified one of the accomplices as Patty Hearst. Shortly before the bank robbery, the FBI had gotten its first decent lead on Hearst in a while. Walter Scott, brother of Jack Scott, who stayed with Hearst at the Pennsylvania farmhouse, spilled the farmhouse location and story to the FBI when he needed money. The FBI quickly located the farmhouse, but the trail proved to be five months cold and, after a couple of discussions with Scott and his wife, FBI interest in Jack Scott faded. They had decided he no longer had good connections with the SLA.

Randolph Hearst's interest did not fade. He met with Jack Scott numerous times in trying to arrange a deal for Patty's return. The FBI, in turn, watched the comings and goings. Randolph would not tell agents what was happening, but Catherine, Patty's mother, obliged. Suddenly, it seemed to the FBI, Jack Scott was indeed still in touch with the SLA, and it might be possible he would lead agents to them.

The FBI needed something. Over the

months it had spot-checked more than 30,000 people in the San Francisco area and through the length of the investigation had used 8500 agents. Tips had been pursued overseas. All that effort had accomplished nothing. The FBI started rechecking people with even vague connections to Jack Scott, looking for the person who might have introduced him to SLA members.

The key would turn out to be a red Volkswagen neighbors had noticed at the Pennsylvania farmhouse hideout. Agents checked on it when they first discovered the farmhouse and they found it was registered to a friend of Scott's. When they rechecked during the summer of 1975, the registration had been changed to a Kathy Soliah. They found her in San Francisco.

Agents started watching her. At about that time, Soliah became mediator between Hearst, who was growing disenchanted with the SLA, and Bill Harris, who became the leader after the 1974 shootout. Agents noticed that Soliah was going back and forth between two houses, neither of which was her own residence. The agents started watching one of the houses, that of Bill and Emily Harris. They recognized Bill Harris, also known as General Teko, and on 18 September 1975 moved in and arrested the couple outside their house. They expected to find Patty inside. They didn't. Then someone thought of checking the other house Soliah had visited. Wendy Yoshimura, who had been living with Hearst, answered the door. They found Hearst trying to hide in a closet. Hearst was convicted for her urban guerrilla activities and she served a short sentence.

Kelley retired from the director's job in January 1978. Months before the retirement, he told a luncheon crowd in Kansas City that his biggest accomplishment was to install within the FBI the ability to make constructive changes, something that had not existed during Hoover's years. He also expressed some bitterness that the media had paid no attention to that progress, but had written reams about anything negative. His was a common complaint about the media, although a complaint that was almost never heard during the Hoover years.

LEFT: FBI Director Clarence Kelley in 1977. He retired in January 1978.

CHAPTER EIGHT

TODAY'S FBI

With the approach of the 1980s, the leadership of the FBI passed from policemen to judges. The first federal jurist to head the country's top law enforcement agency was a Republican hired by a Democrat. Judge William H Webster, of the 8th US Circuit Court of Appeals, was sworn in as the bureau's director on 31 January 1978. Webster was President Jimmy Carter's second choice for the job, tapped after US District Judge Frank M Johnson, a Southern civil rights pioneer, declined the post because of poor health. Attorney General Griffin Bell called the selection of the Missouri jurist 'the best appointment of the Carter administration.'

Webster, although serving at the pleasure of the president, was the first director to be named to a 10-year term created by an act of Congress in an effort to depoliticize the post. He was rapidly confirmed by the Senate and assumed control of an agency suffering sagging morale and a tarnished public image. Concerned that the bureau had become overly sensitive to media coverage, Webster lowered the volume on the FBI's press relations. 'We have no friends. We have no enemies [in the news media],' he said. 'That's out the window. We don't engage in hyperbole anymore.' Webster also announced the goal of opening the agent ranks to more women and minorities, a movement that had started under Gray before Watergate ended his brief stay.

Equipped with a broad-based reputation for integrity and a demonstrated willingness to work (and play – he wielded a mean tennis racket against the likes of Ted Kennedy and William Proxmire) with Congress, Webster moved swiftly to restore the morale and reputation of the agency that had suffered from the emerging scandals of the Hoover

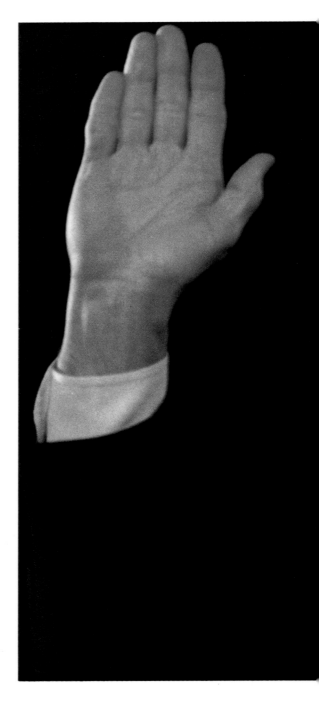

years. He voiced solidarity with the agency's 20,000 employees. 'I came in with the idea of leading the bureau, not as some Justice Department army of occupation.'

Webster loosened the bureau's long-standing tradition of harsh punishment for agents' sexual relationships outside of marriage. No longer would extramarital or pre-marital sex result in automatic dismissal from the bureau. He also eased slightly the old rules concerning marijuana use and homosexuality, and developed the FBI's first clear-cut guidelines on such conduct. While continuing to ban practicing homosexuals from bureau jobs, Webster called for the latest scientific data about homosexuality. Saying he would not tolerate drug use in the bureau, he chose to fine and place on

probation an agent who admitted having smoked pot in college. The man would have been fired immediately in the Hoover years. 'We are still revising a very extensive over-haul of our discipline procedures to build in more due process and put more emphasis on honesty and integrity rather than on private lifestyles,' Webster said in 1979.

If lifestyles were changing for FBI agents, the dangers of their work under Webster's direction were as real and unchanging as in the heyday of the classic G-Men of the 1930s. Thursday, 10 August 1979, was a grim day even for an agency not unfamiliar with violent death. On that summer day, three FBI special agents were killed in the line of duty in two unrelated shootings.

Johnnie Oliver, special agent in the

BELOW: FBI Director William Webster takes the oath in April 1987, saying he will do all that he can to earn the trust of Congress.

ABOVE: Drawing depicting an FBI agent posing as an Arab meeting with one of the congressmen targeted in the agency's bribery investigation, Abscam.

RIGHT: Videotaped evidence of undercover FBI agent Anthony Ameruso offering Rep. Michael Myers a bribe. The tape was aired by the major television networks in October 1980.

bureau's Cleveland office, was gunned down in a public housing project as he tried to arrest 19-year-old Melvin Bay Guyon, a fugitive wanted in Illinois. A few hours later, special agents James Porter and Charles Elmore were shot to death in the FBI office in El Centro, California, by a social worker who had made an appointment to discuss his 'dissatisfaction with the government' concerning the denial of his Freedom of Information Act request for FBI file information. Social worker James Maloney had entered the office with a shotgun stashed in a garment bag and a six-shot revolver. Maloney killed the two unsuspecting agents with the shotgun, then turned the handgun on himself and fired a fatal shot into his mouth.

While some aspects of life and death in the bureau were unchanged from the Hoover era, the times were definitely changing in many ways. Although he insisted he felt 'no personal obligation to defend or attack the past,' Webster seemed to make a symbolic split with the bureau's controversial legacy when he removed a bust of J Edgar Hoover from the director's office. More concrete changes came in Webster's redirected investigative emphasis, moving the focus from bank heists to white collar crime, drug trafficking and espionage. 'Effective law enforcement is not static. It is dynamic,' he said. He stepped up the investigative use of electronic technology, which figured prominently in the two biggest cases cracked during his watch: Abscam and the Walker spy ring.

In February 1980, the bureau's biggest and most celebrated political corruption investigation, Abscam, made its startling television premiere. Agents posing as representatives of an Arab sheik paid out almost half a million dollars in cash to members of Congress and other public officials as video cameras rolled.

The probe was not initially aimed at Congress but started as a loosely coordinated effort by US attorneys and strike force chiefs in New Jersey, New York, Pennsylvania and Florida. Webster approved redirecting the focus of the investigation as a pattern of political corruption began to emerge. A United States senator and seven members of the House of Representatives, as well as a

BELOW: This home in the Georgetown section of Washington was the meeting place of undercover agents and seven congressmen.

ABOVE: Special agents training at the indoor firing range at the FBI Academy in Quantico, Virginia.

OPPOSITE: Agents training in boxing at the academy.

RIGHT: A special agent on an outdoor firing range at the academy.

RIGHT: Congressman John Jenrette of South Carolina being consoled by his family in November 1980. Jenrette was convicted of bribery charges connected with Abscam.

OPPOSITE: Representative John Murphy of New York complains of the FBI releasing Abscam tapes during his bid for re-election.

BELOW: Senator Harrison Williams of New Jersey attempts to defend himself against bribery allegations.

number of private attorneys and state and local officials, were implicated as a result of the video-taped sting operation.

In addition to hundreds of thousands of dollars in cash, the elaborate investigative scheme involved such 'covers' as a large yacht manned by an FBI crew, an ocean resort condominium, a Washington townhouse and several private planes. Abscam critics called the operation entrapment and condemned the role of informant Melvin Weinberg, a self-confessed con man. The bureau insisted its agents did not seek out politicians but were led to them by lawyers boasting they could buy off public officials. The FBI would be involved in a number of other stings, and all of these would bring cries of entrapment, the standard defense in such an operation.

Among those convicted in Abscam were Representatives John M Murphy, D-New York; Michael J Myers, D-Pennsylvania; Frank Thompson Jr, D-New Jersey; Raymond F Lederer, D-Pennsylvania; John Jenrette, D-South Carolina; Richard Kelly, R-Florida; and Senator Harrison A Williams Jr. At least 12 other local and state officials, including a whole gaggle of Philadelphia officials, also were convicted of various charges. All those convicted appealed their decisions on up the ladder of courts; all convictions eventually were upheld.

Accusations of entrapment were harder for the bureau to shrug off in the highly publicized 'sting' operation that led to cocaine conspiracy indictments against auto executive John Z DeLorean in 1982. When the case went to a federal jury in Los Angeles in August 1984, DeLorean was acquitted on all eight counts because jurors believed the government had entrapped him in a drug set-up with promises of money to save his failing car company.

Attorney General William French Smith expressed disappointment in the DeLorean verdict, but said the decision would not deter the federal government from using more 'sting' operations. 'Undercover operations are one of the most effective and successful investigative tools available today in the war against organized crime, drug trafficking, bribery and public corruption,' Smith said. 'In many cases, it is the only method of combating these evils.'

Webster pointed out that the government had gathered enough evidence for the trial judge to let the case go to the jury. 'I respect the decision of the jury. That's what our system is all about.' Webster added, however, that the government's guidelines for undercover work would be reviewed to 'see whether in any particular cases, this one for example, we could have done it better'

either in the courtroom or in the course of the investigation. Webster said sting operations are usually complicated and difficult to execute.

Some bureau officials, speaking anonymously to the press, criticized the FBI and federal drug enforcement agents in the DeLorean case for violating agency policies against altering their records and paperwork, a fact brought out in court by lawyers for the auto entrepreneur.

OPPOSITE: John Z DeLorean at a press conference in February 1982.

LEFT: Attorney General William French Smith was disappointed by the DeLorean verdict. All cocaine conspiracy charges were dropped when jurors decided that DeLorean had been set up.

BELOW: Auto magnate John DeLorean enters federal court in April 1983 for a hearing to have his $5 million bail lowered.

OPPOSITE TOP: President Ronald Reagan in March 1981 just split seconds before John Hinckley attempts to assassinate him.

OPPOSITE BOTTOM: The ensuing turmoil caused by the shooting.

BOTTOM LEFT: Convicted spy Michael Walker is driven away from Federal Court in Baltimore in November 1986 after being sentenced to 25 years in prison for espionage.

BOTTOM RIGHT: Spy ring leader John Walker, left, on his way to a 1985 hearing on charges of selling US military secrets to the Soviets.

During the Reagan years, FBI domestic intelligence gathering began to expand again. It had been hindered by a change in federal laws in 1976. One of the primary reasons for the FBI resuming its domestic efforts was the attempted assassination of the president himself.

On 30 March 1981, John W Hinckley Jr, a mentally disturbed Texas native, ambushed the president in Washington. Reagan and three others, including White House Press Secretary James S Brady, were wounded. Hinckley was arrested at the scene, and the FBI set to work trying to determine if Hinckley had acted alone. Bureau investigators sooned uncovered a bizarre background to the shootings. Hinckley had attempted to kill Reagan to impress actress Jodie Foster, with whom he was infatuated. That motive and other evidence led the bureau to conclude that the shootings were not the result of a conspiracy.

Less than five months after the shootings, a Treasury Department report concluded that the Secret Service had been restricted in protecting the president by 1976 reforms that had limited the FBI's domestic surveillance. The report suggested that the limitations on the FBI be loosened, and some of them were.

The FBI's counterespionage work continued in the 1980s with the cracking of one of the most damaging spy rings in United States history. On 19 May 1985, John A Walker Jr, a balding and bookish-looking retired Navy submariner, drove from his Norfolk, Virginia, home to Montgomery County, Maryland, to dump some bags of garbage.

Tucked in one grocery sack among empty bottles and a soap wrapper was a repair manual for the USS *Blue Ridge*, one of the Navy's two amphibious command ships.

Disregarding the 'No Hunting' sign on a nearby post, FBI agents, who had observed the trash drop from on land and in the air, picked up the classified Navy document before it could be collected by a Soviet agent. The next morning, at a Rockville, Maryland, motel, agents picked up Walker, who for 17 years had masterminded a family spy ring that fed United States military secrets to the Soviets. Walker's was an operation former Navy Secretary John Lehman called 'the most costly act of espionage in the history of our country.'

Before his estranged wife informed on him, Walker, his brother Arthur, son Michael and friend Jerry Whitworth, all Navy communications specialists, had passed along enough cryptographic codes to enable the Soviets to decode thousands of secret military messages. Ship repair documents, such as those in the Maryland trash drop, could let the Soviet Union know how much damage would be required to sink US vessels.

Among evidence used to convict the Walkers of espionage were tapes from FBI wiretaps authorized by the US Foreign Intelligence Surveillance Court, a special unit set up in 1978 to approve electronic surveillance in national security investigations. John and Arthur Walker are serving life in federal prison. Michael Walker was given a 25-year term. Whitworth was sentenced to 365 years in prison and fined $410,000.

The bureau was less proud of busting another celebrated Soviet spy, Richard W Miller. This 'collar' was less satisfying to the agents because it involved one of the bureau's own; Miller had been an FBI special agent for 20 years. An agent with the counterintelligence section of the FBI's Los Angeles office, Miller conspired with Russian emigres Nikola and Svetlana Ogorodnikov to pass classified documents to the Soviet Union. Miller claimed he was merely trying to revive his flagging FBI career by infiltrating the Soviet KGB on his own. Prosecutors in the case thought otherwise. They said he was a bitter man interested only in revenge, sex and money. In sentencing Miller to two life terms plus 50 years, US District Judge David Kenyon expressed the hope that Miller would 'not walk again in this country as a free man.'

Webster called the Miller case 'an aberration on the proud record of patriotic and dedicated service of thousands of special agents throughout our history.' He pointed out that it was FBI special agents who brought Miller to justice. It was, in fact, the first time in the history of the bureau that an agent, despite the many opportunities open

to them, had been charged with betraying his country. While the Miller case marked a low point in the bureau's history, the new director tried to take some comfort from the fact that the compromise of an FBI agent was remarkable because it was such an anomaly.

Webster and the FBI lightly brushed against the Iran-Contra scandal when the director told congressional investigators he had read an October 1986 Justice Department memorandum questioning the activities of National Security Council aide Oliver North. During confirmation hearings on his nomination as director of the Central Intelligence Agency, Webster told a Senate panel he had read, initialed, then forgotten about the memo. 'I didn't see any danger signals at the time,' Webster said, although he admitted being worried by North's influence at the NSC. '[North] was a very gung-ho person with tunnel vision, results-oriented, without a broader gauge of the implications of what he was doing.'

Webster offered the services of the FBI to assist Attorney General Edwin Meese in his investigation of the Iran-Contra arms deal, but Meese declined. The brush with the

scandal did not appear to damage Webster's reputation for integrity, nor impede his confirmation as CIA director.

When William Webster left the bureau after nine years to take charge of the CIA, Attorney General Edwin Meese said the Reagan Administration was looking for a Webster 'clone' to pick up the reins at the FBI. The agency director's chair was to go to another tough, ramrod-straight rule-stickler from the federal bench: United States District Judge William Steele Sessions of San Antonio, Texas.

In September 1987, the United States Senate confirmed Sessions on a 90-0 vote for a 10-year term as FBI director. Illness twice delayed Sessions' swearing-in. The Judge waited out a bleeding ulcer – and followed the soap opera-like confirmation hearings of United States Supreme Court nominee Robert Bork – in a hospital bed. Sessions finally took charge of the agency in November 1987.

Born the son of a Disciples of Christ minister in Fort Smith, Arkansas, Sessions was graduated from Baylor Law School and practiced law in Waco, Texas for 11 years before joining the Justice Department in Washington as head of one section of the

LEFT: Attorney General Edwin Meese at a 1986 news conference.

OPPOSITE: Lt Col Oliver North takes the oath before testifying at the Iran/Contra hearings in July 1987.

BELOW: President Reagan announced in July 1987 that William Sessions, center, a federal judge from Texas, would replace William Webster, left, as head of the FBI.

Criminal Division in 1969. He was in charge of the prosecution of draft evasion, pornography, election fraud and Foreign Corrupt Practices Act cases.

He went to San Antonio in 1972 as US Attorney, was named to the federal bench there in 1974, and became the chief judge of the district in 1980.

Like Judge Webster before him, Judge Sessions quietly announced his intention to aim high-tech investigations at computerized criminals, racketeers, terrorists and spies. 'I covet for the bureau greater and enhanced capability in every area where electronics and automation capabilities take us,' he said. One of the first federal judges to computerize his court, Sessions said he wants to continue to bring the FBI into the electronics age. 'To me it's absolutely essential in an investigative agency that we have, if we can afford it, the best that's available at the cutting edge of the state of the art. We need to have all the in-house capability we can handle.'

Intensive FBI computerization has made government watchdogs jittery in recent years. The FBI, of course, is not the only tar-

get of those fears. The computer can be intrusive if used without checks, and the potential abuse of the new technology raises the old fears of liberty suffering at the hands of the administrators of justice.

On other technological fronts, the FBI is often in the lead. In the last couple of years the famed bureau laboratories have moved criminal investigation into the computer age. Lab workers can tell whether a hair found at a crime scene came from a man or a woman, and lasers can lift fingerprints from the inside of gloves.

Sessions has also voiced his desire to increase the investigative pressure on white-collar criminals by stepping up the use of Racketeer Influenced and Corrupt Organizations – or RICO – laws to go after the financial assets of criminal organizations.

His colleagues say Sessions' penchant for personal involvement, exacting standards and playing by the rules will be good for the FBI. Gerald Goldstein, general counsel of the Texas Civil Liberties Union, who called Sessions 'as fair as any judge I've ever seen,' said Sessions is well-suited for his role at the bureau. 'He's going to be a good cop.' Gold-

BELOW: Attorney General Meese presents new FBI Director William Sessions with his badge and identification card in November 1987.

LEFT: The J Edgar Hoover Building on Pennsylvania Avenue in Washington, DC.

BELOW: FBI special agents undergoing classroom training at the national academy.

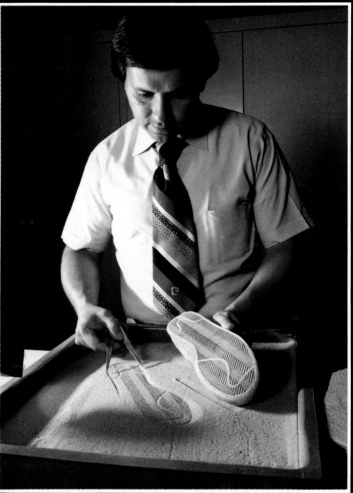

TOP LEFT: A Visual Information Specialist works in the bureau's Special Projects Section.

ABOVE: A seriology examiner removes a bloodstain for chemical analysis.

LEFT: The crime lab compares shoe prints from the scene of a crime.

OPPOSITE TOP: Evidence analysis at the FBI crime lab.

OPPOSITE BOTTOM: A seriologist examining a blood sample at the FBI crime lab.

RIGHT: Luz Yaneth Alfaro of the non-governmental Human Rights Commission alleges in a 1986 news conference that the Catholic Church and US Solidarity groups are backing guerrilla activity in El Salvador.

BELOW: New Jersey authorities display weapons and literature taken during a 1984 raid of the quarters of suspected revolutionaries in Cherry Hill, New Jersey.

stein said. 'He'll make them play by the rules. He understands conflicts of interests and the limits placed by Congress on the FBI. He's not going to play games with that sort of thing.' Added a prosecutor who knows Sessions: 'He won't change the general thrust of the bureau, but he will make them do it the right way. They'll have to cross every "t" and dot every "i."'

Sessions aims to keep as a high priority checks on domestic terrorism. While saying he is concerned about protecting First Amendment rights for political activists, Sessions warned that when free speech 'becomes violent and coercive, it becomes concern for investigative agencies.'

Before Sessions could settle into his chair, a scandal broke over the bureau's six-year domestic surveillance of opponents of the Reagan Administration's Central America policy, testing his theory on First Amendment rights. Although more than 150 organizations were named in FBI files made public by a New York civil rights group, the focal point of the probe was the Committee in Solidarity with the People of El Salvador, or CISPES, which was suspected of possible terrorist ties.

The bureau's conduct of two undercover probes of the organization drew critical comparison between the CISPES investiga-

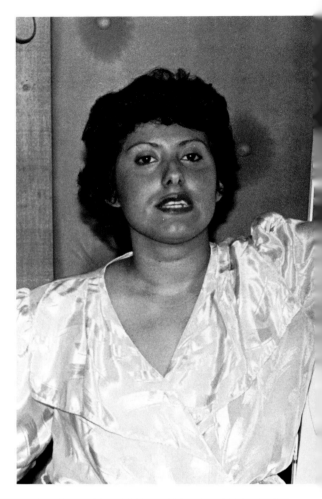

rorism. The FBI later concluded that Varelli fed the bureau 'disinformation and misinformation.' 'The issues we are talking about go to the very heart of the confidence the American people have in the FBI,' said Senator Howard Metzenbaum, an Ohio Democrat and member of the Senate Intelligence Committee that studied the matter behind closed doors.

The FBI investigation of CISPES ended in June 1985, after a Justice Department review concluded that the group was involved

BELOW: A Salvadorean guerrilla stands watch with his American-made weapon, captured from government forces.

tions and the communist-hunting days of the 1950s that led to restrictions on the FBI's investigations into political activities. The first time the FBI investigated CISPES it suspected the group was operating as a foreign front for communists. The second time, it suspected the organization of engaging in terrorism and having 'cells' of members planning to commit violence and sabotage.

CISPES leaders admitted supporting the Frente Farabundo Marti de Liberacion Nacional, or FMLN, the communist guerrillas in El Salvador. The FBI reported the organization is responsible for numerous terrorist acts including the May 1983 assassination of Navy Lieutenant Commander Albert A Schaufelberger, a US military advisor in El Salvador. But a CISPES spokesman called FMLN 'a legitimate political organization in El Salvador,' adding, 'if the United States got out of El Salvador, no Americans would be killed.'

In March 1981, the FBI hired a former evangelist from El Salvador, Frank Varelli, to inform on CISPES. For more than three years, Varelli testified before a congressional panel, he told the FBI what it wanted to hear: that the group's activities were directed by guerrillas and that CISPES members were engaged in international ter-

BELOW: An El Salvadorean guerrilla stands guard in front of a post of the ERP, the Popular Revolutionary Army.

BOTTOM LEFT: Grieving for victims of the guerrilla war.

BOTTOM RIGHT: A masked supporter of the Salvadorean Communist Party.

RIGHT: A soldier in the El Salvador Army.

in First Amendment activities, not international terrorism. Sessions, who was called to testify behind the closed doors of the Senate Intelligence Committee, conceded that parts of the investigation may not have been properly directed. But he denied charges from the Center for Constitutional Rights that the surveillance involved hundreds of groups and individuals. He later fired or reprimanded six agents involved in the CISPES investigation.

Rebuilding the integrity of the FBI while steering it into the twenty-first century seems an appropriate chore for a challenge-seeker like William Sessions, an avid mountain climber and would-be space traveler. In early 1986, unsatisfied by earthly challenges, he applied to the National Aeronautics and Space Administration in hopes of being one of the civilians chosen for a space shuttle flight. Sessions may yet get his turn in a spaceship. But for now, he has his hands full, holding the controls of a larger, more powerful craft: the Federal Bureau of Investigation.

ABOVE: Members of the American-trained and -equipped El Salvador Army.

LEFT: An army column ready for action.

PAGE 190: The flag at the Justice Department in Washington, DC flies at half mast in May 1972 in honor of the death of J Edgar Hoover, at the age of 77.

Index

(Numerals in italics indicate illustrations)

191

Acknowledgments

The authors and publisher would like to thank the following people who helped in the preparation of this book: Design 23, who designed it; Jean Martin, who edited it; Rita Longabucco and Donna Cornell Muntz, who did the picture research; and Florence Norton, who prepared the index.

Picture Credits

The Bettmann Archive, Inc: 6, 7, 14(bottom), 16, 17(top), 21(top), 22(bottom), 24, 30(top), 41, 43, 44, 45(top, bottom), 46(top, bottom), 50, 54(bottom), 55(bottom), 61(bottom), 62, 64, 69, 78, 80, 81(top), 87(top), 88(top), 100(bottom), 101(bottom), 105(top).
The Bettmann Archive/BBC Hulton: 86(bottom).
The Bettmann Archive/Springer: 75(bottom).
Bison Library: 47, 49(top, bottom), 52(top), 86(top), 124, 127, 145, 156(bottom).
Camera Press: 188-189(all six).
Federal Bureau of Investigation: 2(top, bottom), 3(right), 27(left), 29, 72(top left, bottom left), 143, 170, 171(top, bottom), 183(top, bottom), 184(top left, bottom right, bottom), 185(top, bottom).
Lyndon Baines Johnson Library: 137(top).
John F Kennedy Library: 134(top, bottom), 135(top), 139(top, bottom).
Library of Congress: 8, 9, 20(top), 25(bottom), 30(bottom), 32(top, bottom), 33(bottom).
National Archives: 4, 10(top right, bottom), 13(top), 17(bottom), 18(top, bottom), 19, 21(bottom), 22(top), 26, 27, 28(bottom), 34, 35(top, bottom), 52(bottom), 55(top), 60, 61(top), 73(bottom right), 74(top right), 76(top, bottom), 77(bottom), 79(bottom), 87(bottom), 90(top, bottom), 91, 92, 93, 99(top), 100(top), 101(top), 110, 140, 142(top), 146(top).
National Archives, Nixon Presidential Materials Project: 157(bottom).
New York Public Library Picture Collection: 67(top), 115(bottom), 158(bottom).
UPI/Bettmann Newsphotos: 3(left), 11, 12, 13(left), 14(top), 15(top, bottom), 20(bottom), 23, 25(top), 28(top), 31(top, bottom), 36, 37, 38, 39(top left, bottom left, right), 40, 42, 51, 53(top, bottom), 54(top), 56, 57,

58(top, bottom), 59, 63, 65(top, bottom), 66(left), 66-67(bottom), 68(top right, bottom left), 70, 71(top, bottom), 72-73(bottom), 74(top left), 75(top), 77(top), 79(top), 81(center), 82, 83, 84, 85, 88(bottom), 89, 94, 95, 96, 97, 98, 99(bottom), 102(top, bottom), 103(bottom), 104, 105(bottom left, bottom right), 106, 107, 108-109, 109, 111, 112, 113(top, bottom), 114(top, bottom), 115(top), 116, 117, 118, 119(top, bottom), 120, 121(top, bottom), 123(top, bottom), 125(top, bottom left, bottom right), 126(top, bottom), 128(top, bottom), 129(bottom), 130(top, bottom), 131(top, bottom), 132, 132-133, 137(bottom), 138(top, bottom left, bottom right), 141, 142(bottom), 144(top, bottom), 146(top), 147, 148, 150(top, bottom), 151, 152, 153, 154(top), 154-155(bottom), 155(top, bottom right), 156(top), 157(top), 158(top), 159, 160, 161(top, bottom), 162(top, bottom), 163, 164(top, bottom), 165, 166-167, 168(top, bottom), 169, 172(top, bottom), 173, 174, 175(top, bottom), 176(left, right), 178, 179, 180, 181(top, bottom), 182, 186-187(top), 186(bottom), 187, 190.
US Senate Historical Office: 10(top left), 33(top), 81(bottom).
The White House/Michael Evans: 177(top, bottom).
WW: 103(top), 129(top), 135(bottom), 136.